Structured Query Language
SQL

*"SQL from Beginner to Intermediate.
The Latest Guide to Mastering SQL
(2020 Edition)"*

JOHNNY PAGE

TABLE OF CONTENTS

Disclaimer 1

CHAPTER ONE: SUMMARY ON THE BASICS OF
SQL 4

What is SQL? 4

Where is next? 13

SQL commands: 16

CHAPTER TWO 18

SQL SELECT 18

SQL SELECT statement 18

Alias field names 24

CHAPTER THREE 33

SQL WHERE 33

What is the WHERE clause? 33

Find the lines using a simple equality 35

Find lines that fulfil two conditions 36

Find the lines using the comparison operator 37

Find lines that meet one of the two conditions 38

Find lines with a value between two values 39

In the list of advantages, find the lines that have a
value 40

Find lines whose rate contain a string 41

We could use the WHERE clause. 49

CHAPTER FOUR 51

SQL joins using WHERE or ON 51

Filtered in the ON clause 51

Filtered in the WHERE clause 53

Refine your SQL skills 54

The syntax of the WHERE clause in SQL is as
follows: 55

CHAPTER FIVE 62

  FROM in SQL 62

    SQL clause: FROM 62

    Example: a table listed in the FROM clause 63

    Enter the following SQL statement: 64

    Enter the following SQL statement: 66

    Why start with the FROM clause? 68

    FROM more than one table using JOIN 71

CHAPTER SIX 79

  AND in SQL 79

    Update your customers 83

CHAPTER SEVEN 86

  OR in Sql 86

    The syntax for the OR state in SQL is as follows:. 86

CHAPTER EIGHT 93

  The difference between internal and external unions. 93

    The cross joins 94

    Some of the entrance tables are hidden 99

    The relationships 100

    All columns are available after joining 104

    UNION asked 119

    UNION and UNION ALL 122

    Viewpoints 123

    Data combination with UNION 132

    Union 134

    Union all 135

    How to use SQL Union with queries that have a
WHERE clause 142

    SQL UNION ALL using where 149

    SQL UNION table by itself 150

    SQL UNION with different column names 151

    SQL UNION with internal union 151

SQL: Union against Union of all...........................152

How to utilise the SELECT INTO clause and SQL Union 156

How to use SQL Union with WHERE and ORDER BY queries. 157

How to use SQL Union and SQL Pivot................158

UNION deletes duplicate rows............................163

Example: different field names............................167

Explore this example with the data.......................179

Use simple UNION 184

Using SELECT INTO with UNION 186

Using the union of two SELECT statements with ORDER BY 187

Using the UNION of Three SELECT Statements to Show the Effects of ALL and Parentheses 189

Using a simple union 194

Using two SELECT UNION statements with ORDER BY 194

Using two SELECT UNION statements with WHERE and ORDER BY 196

Use the UNION of three SELECT statements to display the effects of ALL and parentheses..........197

SQL JOIN 199

See the following statements: 202

Unbalanced link conditions in database queries...205

CHAPTER NINE...208

Difference between function and stored procedure..208

What is a stored procedure (SP)? 208

Why is a stored procedure useful?........................208

Why do we need a stored procedure?....................209

Why do not we need a stored procedure?..............209

When is the registered process appropriate for us? 210

Stored procedure data.. 210
Comparing Functions and Procedures Stored in SQL
Server 212
CHAPTER TEN 221
SQL Encrypting... 221
Always Encrypted... 221
Transparent Data Encryption (TDE)..................... 225

DISCLAIMER

All intellect contained in this book is given for enlightening and instructive purposes as it were. The creator isn't in any capacity responsible for any outcomes or results that radiate from utilising this material. Worthwhile endeavours have been made to give data that is both precise and viable. However, the creator isn't oriented for the exactness or use/misuse of this data.

due to the information herein, either directly or indirectly. Respective authors own all copyrights not held by the publisher. The information herein is offered for informational purposes solely, and is universal as so. The presentation of the information is without contract or any type of guarantee assurance. The trademarks that are used are without any consent, and the publication of the trademark is without permission or backing by the trademark owner. All trademarks and brands within this book are for clarifying purposes only and are owned by the owners themselves, not affiliated with this document.

CHAPTER ONE
SUMMARY ON THE BASICS OF SQL

What is SQL?

Structured Query Language (SQL) is a specific programming language for querying databases. Most small databases and industrial databases are accessible using SQL statements. SQL is the ANSI and ISO standard. However, many database products that support SQL do so with proprietary standard language extensions. Web applications can use user-supplied inputs to create custom SQL statements for dynamic Web requests.

What is SQL injection?

An SQL injection is a technique that exploits a security vulnerability that occurs in a web application database layer. Weakness is present when the user input is poorly filtered because of literal escape strings embedded in

SQL statements or if the user input is not typed and therefore starts unexpectedly. It is an example of a more general vulnerability class that can occur whenever a programming or scripting language is integrated with another.

"SQL injection" is a subset of uncontrolled/uninfected user input vulnerabilities ("buffer overflows" are different subgroups). The idea is to convert the application so as to execute the unscheduled SQL code. If the form naively creates SQL strings when you move and then runs them, then it's easy to create real surprises.

Many of a company's web servers are compromised only by SQL injection, including by big names that I would not want to mention here, and you can effortlessly search them on the Internet.

What is a blind SQL injection?

This type of attack is called a blind SQL injection attack because the attacker cannot exploit detailed error messages from the server or other sources of application information. Getting the correct SQL syntax is usually the most complex part of the hidden SQL injection process and it can take a lot of trial and error. But by adding more status to the SQL statement and access the results of the Web application, the attacker will eventually determine if the application is vulnerable to

SQL injection.

A blind SQL injection is a particular case that affects the security of web developers or website owners. Although, I may think that everything on the server is strictly protected, but a blind SQL injection attack will quietly play the truth or the consequences on the Web server. This type of attack, despite taking a lot of time, is the major one that provides the most reliable security hole. This is because not only does an attacker receive access, but it also provides him with a considerable amount of knowledge about the database and can potentially access the server's file system. This type of attack is automatic and requires the right amount of configuration in order to succeed. But once you do, it does not take much effort to repeat it.

What is an SQL injection error message?

Web applications often use SQL queries with client-supplied entries in the WHERE clause to retrieve data from the database. When a Web application executes such requests without checking or analysing the information provided by the user to ensure that they are not harmful, SQL injection attacks can occur. When sending unexpected data, an attacker can generate and send SQL queries to a Web application database. The SQL injection vulnerability test is performed by sending application data that produces an invalid SQL query. If the server returns an error message, then this information can be used to attempt uncontrolled access to the database. This is the footing of one of the most successful SQL injection attacks.

Hiding the error messages does not stop the SQL injection attack. What usually happens is that the attacker will use the knowledge gained from the failure of this attack to change tactics. What they are for is a blind injection of SQL.

Why SQL injection?

When a Web application fails to sanitise the user-supplied entry successfully, the attacker can change the construction of the SQL helper statements. When an attacker modifies an SQL statement, the process will run with the same permissions as the component that executed the command. (For example, database server, web application server, web server, etc.). The effect of this attack may allow attackers to gain complete control of the base

When only port 80 is open, your most reliable vulnerability scanner cannot return anything useful, and you ought to know that the administrator always repairs your server, this is the point at which a malicious hacker would become a hacker of the network. An SQL injection is a case of hacking that requires nothing more than port 80 and can work even if the administrator is satisfied. It attacks a web application (such as ASP, JSP, PHP, CGI, etc.) instead of a Web server or services running in the operating system.

SQL injection types:

There are four primary categories of SQL injection attacks in the database layer of a Web application.

1. SQL manipulation: Manipulation is the procedure of modifying SQL statements by using various operations such as UNION. Another way to implement SQL injection using the SQL manipulation method is to change the location of the SQL statement clause to produce different results.

2. Code insertion: Code insertion is the process of inserting new SQL statements or database commands into a vulnerable SQL statement. One of the code injection attacks is to add the SQL Server EXECUTE command to a sensitive SQL statement. This type of attack is only possible if multiple SQL statements are supported per database query.

3. Function Call Injection: The function call injection is the process of inserting multiple database function calls into a vulnerable SQL statement. These function calls

can request the operating system or manipulate data in a database.

4. Buffer overflow: The injection of a calling function causes buffer overflows. Fixes are available for most commercial and open source databases. This type of attack is possible when the server is not being repaired.

SQL injections prevention techniques:

Mitigating the vulnerability to SQL injection would be one of two, i.e. you use stored procedures with called statements or annotations prepared with dynamic SQL commands. Whichever method is adopted; data verification is very essential.

A. Checking the entry.

Data recovery is key. The best way to recover data is to use a collective denial, a regular expression. Write specific filters. Use numbers, numbers, and letters as much as possible. If you need to include punctuation, convert it to HTML encoding. Then, "convert" or "become"> "For example, if a user enters an email address, allow only @, -, And _ with numbers and letters that will only be used after being sent, and then convert to your HTML replacements.

B. Use the prepared statement.

Prepared declarations must be used when stored

procedures cannot be used for any reason, and dynamic SQL commands must be used.

Use the prepared statement to send pre-assembled SQL statements with one or more parameters. The reserved parameters in the prepared declaration are represented by parameters. and they are also called link variables. The prepared statement is usually immune to SQL injection attacks because the database will only use the value of the link variable and will not interpret the contents of the variable in any way. PL / SQL and JDBC provide prepared instructions. Prepared statements should be widely used for safety and performance reasons. vs Use minimum privileges.

Verify that the application user has specific minimum rights on the database server. If the user of the application in the database uses ROOT / SA / dbadmin / dbo in the database; then it should be reconsidered if the user of the application needs such a large amount of privilege or can reduce it. Do not allow the application that's been used to access the stored procedures of the system also allow access to those created by the user. d. Stored procedures.

To protect an application against SQL injection, developers should never allow clients to change the syntax of their SQL statements. The best protection is to isolate the SQL Web application completely. All SQL statements required by the application must be stored in stored procedures and stored on the database server. The application must execute stored procedures using a secured interface such as callable statement of JDBC or Command Object of ADO.

SQL is a language that allows you to work with a database. With SQL, you can insert records, update records, and delete files. You can also make new database objects, such as databases and tables. And you can delete them as well.

The most advanced features includes creating stored procedures (independent scripts), views (pre-prepared queries), and setting permissions for database objects (such as tables, stored procedures, and images).

Although SQL is the American National Standards Institute (ANSI) standard, there are many different versions of SQL. Various database providers have their language variants.

According to the ANSI standard, they must at least support essential commands such as DELETE, INSERT, UPDATE, WHERE, etc. Also, you will find that many service providers have language extensions features that are only compatible with their database system.

Also, Transact-SQL is an extension of the ANSI standard and provides additional functionality.

Use SQL.

To execute SQL queries in this guide, you will need a database management system such as MySQL, Oracle, Microsoft Access, SQL Server, and so on.

If you are unfamiliar with database management systems, check out my Microsoft Access tutorial, my SQL Server tutorial, and my MySQL tutorial.

If you need to create a site with a database containing content, you will usually need the following knowledge:

Server-side scripting language (i.e. ColdFusion, PHP, ASP / .NET).

Database query language (for example, SQL).

Tabular mark-up language and client-side style sheets (for example, HTML / CSS).

Although you may be very involved in SQL, you can also accomplish a lot with a few SQL statements. When using SQL in a location, you will often find or select a record, insert a record, update a record, or delete a record. Fortunately, SQL has commands to perform each of these actions.

We start by learning that SQL stands for Structured Query Language and is the ANSI standard. We then determine the basic SQL syntax, before switching to the SELECT command, which is probably the most used statement.

We learned that there are several keywords and aggregation functions that can be included in SQL statements, such as WHERE, TIP, DISTINCT, and so on. It's all part of DML (Data Management Language).

Then, by covering the INSERT, UPDATE and DELETE statements, we learned that there are different commands in the database which can be hired to perform administration tasks. For example, there are commands to create database objects (CREATE DATABASE, CREATE TABLE, etc.) and controls to modify (or modify) database objects (ALTER DATABASE, ALTER TABLE, etc...). These commands are part of DDL (Data Definition Language).

Where is next?

If you want to learn SQL programming, you must download the database administration system (if you have not already done so) and execute SQL statements. You must also read the database documentation to see the controls, functions, or features of the property. For example, does your database have an automatic programmer? Can a database server connect to a database on another server? How to back up my database system?

Check out my SQL Server Guide to learn how to work with databases on SQL Server. Most tasks on SQL Server can be done using the GUI or using SQL scripts. This is a great chance to test your knowledge of SQL.

What is SQL? SQL means "Structured Query Language" and can be articulated as "SQL" or "Suite." SQL is defined as a query language used to access and modify information in one or more tables and rows of databases.

SQL database design

IBM developed SQL for the first time in 1970. Also, it is the ANSI / ISO standard. It has become the standard universal language used by most relational database management systems (RDBMS). Many of the RDBMS systems are Oracle, Microsoft SQL Server, Sybase, and so on.

Most of them provided deployment extensions, improving their RDBMS system and making it a powerful tool. All of these RDBMS systems use the popular SELECT, UPDATE, DELETE, INSERT, WHERE SQL commands in a similar format.

SQL database table

The SQL database is built from multiple tables. In a company, SQL tables would be used to divide and simplify different business areas: a customer table, one for suppliers, employees, and so on.

SQL database table columns

Each SQL table is composed of several columns, called fields, and is executed at the top of the table. The columns or SQL fields have their contents (object /data/information) defined in the types of characters; as text, date, numeric, integer, length, to list a few.

SQL database table rows

Each line of the SQL table that references the record is in the left column of the table. The SQL record line will contain a data string containing the data corresponding to each column field at the top. Therefore, in the "customer table," each "customer record" would consist of a line with information for the customer identification number, customer name, address, phone, email, etc.

SQL Commands: Some SQL Encoding Instructions?

Some of the SQL commands used in SQL code programming are a SELECT statement, UPDATE statement, INSERT INTO account, DELETE comment, WHERE clause, ORDER BY clause, SQL GROUP BY clause, subquery clauses, unions, views, GROUP functions, indexes, etc.

My SQL database

SQL is a non-procedural English language that processes data in sets of records, instead of one record at a time. Several SQL functions are:

Saving data.

Modify the data.

Recover data.

Change the information.

Delete data.

Create tables and other database objects.

Delete data.

SQL commands:

SQL commands are instructions encoded in SQL statements that are used to communicate with the database in order to perform specific tasks, operations, functions, and queries with data.

SQL commands can be used not only to search the database, but also to perform other functions such as creating tables, adding data to tables, or modifying data, creating data table, and setting permissions for users. SQL commands are grouped into four main categories, depending on their functionality:

Data Definition Language (DDL): These SQL commands are used to create, modify, and delete the structure of database objects. The controls are CREATE, ALTER, DROP, RENAME and TRUNCATE.

Data manipulation language (DML): These SQL commands are used to store, retrieve, modify and delete data.

These data manipulation language commands are SELECT, INSERT, UPDATE, and DELETE.

Transaction Control Language (TCL): These SQL commands are used to manage changes that are affecting the data. These commands are COMMIT, ROLLBACK and SAVEPOINT.

Data Control Language (DCL): These SQL commands are used to secure database objects. These commands are GRANT and REVOKE.

CHAPTER TWO

SQL SELECT

SQL SELECT statement

The most commonly used SQL command is the SELECT entry. The SQL SELECT statement is used to find or retrieve data from the table in a database. The query can extract information from specific columns or all columns of a table. To make a basic SQL SELECT articulation, you should determine the name of the column (s) and the name of the table. The complete query is called the SQL SELECT statement.

Databases store the data for later retrieval. Ever wondered how this is accomplished? The SELECT SQL command does the job.

That's it; get the data from the tables in the database. This is part of the computer language that is responsible for consulting the database.

Syntax SQL SELECT

This is the most used SQL command, and its general syntax is as follows:

SELECTION [DISTINCT | ALL] {* | [fieldExpression [AS newName]} FROM table_name [alias] [condition WHERE] [table_name GROUP BY] [condition HAVING] ORDER BY name_zone (s).

RIGHT HERE

SELECT is an SQL keyword that allows a database to know how to recover data.

[CLASS | ALL] are optional keywords that can be used to adjust the results returned by the SQL SELECT statement. If nothing is specified, ALL is considered the default value.

{* | [fieldExpression [AS newName]} leastways one part must be nominative, "*" all fields of the specified table name are selected, the field expression performs calculations on specified fields, such as adding numbers or merging two sets of fields into one.

FROM table_name is required and must contain at least one table. A comma must separate multiple tables or associated with the keyword JOIN.

OR the requirement is optional, and it can be used to specify criteria in the result set returned by the query.

GROUP BY is used to collect records with the same field values.

The HAVING condition is used to specify criteria when you use the GROUP BY keyword.

ORDER BY is used to determine the sort order of results.

The asterisk is used to select all columns in the table. An example of a simple SELECT statement is similar to the one shown below.

SELECTION * FROM `members`;

The previous statement selects all fields in the member table. The semicolon ends with a comment. This is optional, but it is considered as a good practice to finalise your accounts this way.

Syntax of the SQL SELECT statement:

CHOOSE THE LIST OF COLUMNS FROM THE NAME OF THE TABLE

[WHERE clause]

[GROUP BY clause]

[HAVING clause]

[ORDER BY PROVISION];

Table_name is the figure of the table from which the data is extracted.

Column list contains one or more columns from which data is retrieved.

The code in parentheses is optional.

Data database details table;

FIRST_NAME LAST_NAME gets the subsets.

100 Rahul Sharma 10 Cricket Science.

101 Anjali Bhagwat 12 Mathematics Football.

102 Stephen Fleming 09 Cricket Science.

103Shekar Gowda 18 Badminton Math.

104 Priya Chandra 15 The shah economy.

NOTE: These database tables are used here to explain SQL commands better. Tables can have other columns and different data.

For example, consider the student details table. To select the name of all students, the query will be:

CHOOSE the name of student details;

SELECTION instructions: syntax.

NOTE: SQL commands are case-sensitive. The previous SELECT statement can also be written as

"Select the name of student details;"

You can also download data from multiple columns. For example, choose the name of each student.

CHOOSE first and last name, DE student details;

You can also use clauses such as WHERE, GROUP BY, HAVING, ORDER BY with a SELECT statement. We will discuss these commands in the following chapters.

NOTE: Only SELECT and FROM comments are required in the SQL SELECT command other clauses such as WHERE, PO ORDER, PO GROUP, MUST be optional.

How to use aspect in the SQL SELECT statement?

Expressions combine many arithmetic operators and can be used in the SELECT, WHERE and ORDER BY clauses of SELECT SQL statements.

Here we explain how to use expressions in an SQL SELECT statement. When using the terms of the WHERE clause and PO ORDER, they will be described in their sections.

Operators are measured in a specific order of precedence

when multiple arithmetic operators are used in an expression. The qualification order is in parentheses, division, multiplication, addition and subtraction. The scope is carried out from left to right.

SELECTION Sample report?

If we wanted to display the first and last name of the employee together, an SQL selection statement would be presented.

SELECT surname and first name + " + name of the worker;

Departure:

name_name + " + name

Rahul Sharma

Anjali Bhagwat

Stephen Fleming

Shekar Gowda

Priya Chandra

You can also add aliases as follows.

CHOOSE first name + " + last name AS employee name;

Departure:

nom_emp

Rahul Sharma

Anjali Bhagwat

Stephen Fleming

Shekar Gowda

Priya Chandra

Alias field names

The previous example returned the union code as the field call for our results. Imagine we want to use a more descriptive field call in our result set. To do this, we would use the column alias name. Here is the basic syntax for the column alias name.

SELECT `column_name | value | expression `[AS]` alias_name`;

RIGHT HERE

"SELECT` column name | value | expression" "Is an ordinary SELECT entry that can be a column name, a value, or a phrase."

"[AS]" is an optional keyword preceding the alias name that indicates the expression, value, or name of the field that will be returned.

"alias_name`" is the name of the alias we want to return in the result as the field name.

Main query with a more meaningful column name.

CHOOSE Concat (`title`, '(', 'director', ')') AS 'Concat', 'year_released` FROM` movies`;

Get a list of members that shows the year of birth.

Suppose we wanted to get a list of all members showing the number of members, the full names, and the year of birth. We can use the LEFT string purpose to retrieve the year of delivery from the date of delivery. The script below helps us do that.

CHOOSE `member_number`, ` full name ', LEFT (`date_life`, 4) AS` year_from` FROM members;

RIGHT HERE.

"LEFT (` date_of_birth`, 4) "The LEFT string function accepts a birth date as a parameter and returns only four characters to the left.

"AS` year_of_birth`" is the name of the alias column that will appear in our results. Note that the AS keyword is optional, you can skip it, and the query will continue to work.

SQL using MySQL Workbench.

Now, we will use the MySQL desktop to generate a script that will show all the field names in our category table.

1. Right-click on the category table. Click on "Select lines - limit of 1000."

2. MySQL Workbench will automatically create an SQL query and paste it into the editor.

3. The result of the inquiry will be shown.

Why use the SELECT SQL command with MySQL Workbench?

You may be wondering now why the SQL SELECT command allows you to write data from a database when you can use a tool such as the MySQL desktop to get the same results without knowing the SQL language. Of course, this is possible, but learning how to use the SELECT command gives you more flexibility and control over SQL SELECT statements.

The MySQL desktop is in the QBE category of the "Query for example" tool. The intention is to help generate faster SQL statements in order to increase user productivity.

Learning the SQL SELECT command can allow you to create complex queries that are not easily generated using a query tool such as MySQL Workbench.

To improve productivity, you can generate a code using a MySQL desktop and customise it to your needs. This can only happen if you know how SQL statements work!

The SQL SELECT keyword is used to enter data from a database and it is the most used command.

The purest form has the syntax "SELECT * FROM table Name;"

Expressions can also be used in the selection command. Example "SELECT PRICE AND SALES PRICE."

The SQL SELECT command may have other optional parameters such as WHERE, PO GROUP, HAVING, PO ORDER. They will be discussed later.

The MySQL panel can help you develop SQL statements, execute, and generate results in the same window.

The SELECT statement is probably the most used in SQL. Just find the data from the database

SELECTION * OF INDIVIDUAL;

This SQL SELECT statement attempts to retrieve all columns from a table called Individual.

How do we know that you are trying to select all the columns? Since you use an asterisk (*). This is a quick way to choose all columns: it's much easier than writing the names of all columns (especially if there are many columns).

Of course, this SQL SELECT statement assumes that there is a table named Individual. If it did not exist, an error would be created.

You can choose from several tables. To do this, separate each table with a comma. You must also evaluate references to columns by putting the name of the table in front, separated by a dot.

SQL statement.

We will select both the individual table and the occupied table. We will classify prefixed column names with the name of their table and their period.

SELECTION * individual, profession.

WHERE Individual. First Name = 'Homer'

I Individual. IndividualId = Occupation. IndividualId;

Show fewer columns.

If you do not need to display all the columns, you can only select the columns that interest you. This is functional programming practise and the more columns you have to restore your program, the more it will affect your performance.

To display only the columns that interest you, replace the asterisk (*) with a comma-separated list of column names.

SQL statement.

CHOOSE IndividualId, last name, username.

From the individual.

WHERE First Name = 'Homer';

Select is the most used statement in SQL. The SQL SELECT statement retrieves data from a database. We can bring the whole table or according to certain specific rules. The returned data is stored in the results table. This result table is also called the result set.

With SELECT statements in the SELECT clause, we specify the columns that we want to display in the query result and, optionally, the column headings we want to see above the results table.

The selection clause is the first clause and it is one of the last provisions of the select statement evaluated by the database server. The reason is that before determining what to include in the final result set, we need to know all the possible columns that can be included in the last result set.

Basic syntax:

SELECTION of columns1, column2 of OF file name.

column1, column2: field names of the table.

table_name: where do we want to go.

This query will return all rows in the table with column1, column2.

To retrieve a complete table or all fields from a table:

SELECTION * FROM table_name;

Query to extract the ROLL_NO, NAME, AGE field from the Student table:

SELECT ROLL_NO, NAME, OLD FROM PUPILS;

The SELECT statement extracts the data from the database.

The data is returned in a table structure called a result set.

SELECT is the most commonly used action in the database.

Syntax SQL SELECT.

The general syntax is as follows:

SELECT column names

FROM table-name

To select all columns to use *

SELECTION *

FROM table-name

SQL SELECT examples

Problem: List all clients

SELECTION *

Client

Results: 91 records.

Id First Name Last Name, Country.

1 Maria Anders Berlin Germany 030-0074321.

2 Ana Trujillo Mexico D.F. Mexico (5) 555-4729.

3 Antonio Moreno, Mexico DF Mexico (5) 555-3932.

4 Thomas Hardy London U K (171) 555-7788.

5 Christina Berglund Luleå Sweden 0921-12 34 65.

BUYER

ID card

Last name

Last name

1 C

Country

Phone number

Problem: Indicate the name, first name and city of all customers.

SELECTION Surname, first name, city.

Client

Results: 91 records.

Name City

Maria Anders, Berlin.

Ana Trujillo, Mexico D.F.

Antonio Moreno, Mexico D.F.

Thomas Hardy, London.

Christina Berglund. Lulea.

CHAPTER THREE

SQL WHERE

What is the WHERE clause?

We examine how to query data from a database using the SELECT statement from the previous tutorial. The SELECT statement returned all the results from the database table accessed.

However, we may want to limit the results of the query to a specific state and the SQL WHERE clause is useful in such situations.

WHERE is the syntax clause?

The basic syntax of the WHERE clause, when used in the SELECT command, is as follows.

CHOOSE * FROM THE TABLE WE HAVE O the condition;

RIGHT HERE.

An introduction to the SQL Server WHERE clause.

When you use the SELECT statement to write data to a table, you get all the rows in that table, which is quite unnecessary because the application can only process one row or rows at a time.

To obtain tables from a table that satisfies one or more conditions, use the WHERE clause as follows:

SELECT

Select_list

IZ

Table_name

Or

Condición_búsqueda;

In the WHERE clause, you stipulate a search condition to filter the rows returned by the FROM clause. The WHERE clause returns only rows that set TRUE to the search query.

A search term is a logical expression or a combination of several logical expressions. In SQL, a logical expression is often named a predicate.

Note that SQL Server uses a three-line predicate logic in which a logical expression can be evaluated as TRUE, FALSE, or UNKNOWN. The WHERE clause will not return any rows in which a predicate will be evaluated as FALSE or UNKNOWN.

Find the lines using a simple equality

The following statement retrieves all products with a category ID 1:

SELECT

Product ID

Product Name,

Category_id,

MODELO_AÑO,

Price list

IZ

Produccion.productos

Or

Category_id = 1

ORDER BY

List_price DESC;

Find lines that fulfil two conditions

The proceed example returns products that meets two requirements: a category ID is one, and a template is 2018. Use logical operator I to combine the two conditions.

SELECT

Product ID

Product Name,

Category_id,

MODELO_AÑO,

Price list

IZ

Produccion.productos

Or

Category_id = 1 and model_year = 2018

ORDER BY

List_price DESC;

Find the lines using the comparison operator

The following statement finds products priced above $ 300 and the model is 2018.

SELECT

Product ID

Product Name,

Category_id,

MODELO_AÑO,

Price list

IZ

Produccion.productos

Or

List_price> 300 AND model_year = 2018

ORDER BY

List_price DESC;

Find lines that meet one of the two conditions

The following query searches for products with a price higher than 3,000 or a 2018 template. Each product that fits one of these conditions are included in the result set.

SELECT

Product ID

Product Name,

Category_id,

MODELO_AÑO,

Price list

IZ

Produccion.productos

Or

List_price> 3000 OR model_year = 2018

ORDER BY

List_price DESC;

Note that the OR operator has been used to combine predicates.

Find lines with a value between two values

The following statement finds products with prices between 1,899 and 1,999.99:

SELECT

Product ID

Product Name,

Category_id,

MODELO_AÑO,

Price list

IZ

Produccion.productos

Or

Price_list BETWEEN 1899.00 AND 1999.99

ORDER BY

List_price DESC;

In the list of advantages, find the lines that have a value

The following example uses an IN operator to search for a product with a list price of 299.99 or 466.99 or 489.99.

SELECT

Product ID

Product Name,

Category_id,

MODELO_AÑO,

Price list

IZ

Produccion.productos

Or

List_ amount IN (299.99, 369.99, 489.99)

ORDER BY

List_price DESC;

Find lines whose rate contain a string

The following example uses the LIKE operator to search for a product named Cruiser string:

SELECT

Product ID

Product Name,

Category_id,

MODELO_AÑO,

Price list

IZ

Produccion.productos

Or

_product name AS '% Cruiser%'.

ORDER BY

Price list;

"SELECT * FROM table Name" is a standard SELECT statement.

"WHERE" is the keyword that limits our result set from the selection query and "condition" is the filter that will be applied to the results. The screen can be a range, a single value, or a subset.

Let's look at a practical example.

Suppose we wanted to get the details of a member table concerning number 1, we would use the following script to do it.

SELECTION * FROM `members` WHERE` member number` = 1;

WHERE the clause is combined with the logical operator - Y

The WHERE clause, when used with the AND logical operator, executes only if ALL the specified filter criteria are met.

Now let's take a concrete example: Suppose we want to get a list of all category of two films released in 2017, we would use the scenario presented below.

SELECTION * FROM `movies` WHERE` category_id` = 2 AND` year separated` = 2008;

Running the previous script in the MySQL workgroup with "myflixdb" produces the following results.

Film_id director title year_electedcategory_id.

Forget Sarah Marshal Nicholas Stoller 2008 2.

WHERE the clause is combined with - OR the logical operator.

The WHERE clause, when used with the OR operator, executes only if some or all of the specified filter criteria are met.

The following script gets all Category 1 or Category 2 movies.

SELECTION * FROM `movies` WHERE` category_id` = 1 OR category_id` = 2;

Running the previous script in the MySQL workgroup with "myflixdb" produces the following results.

Film_id director title year_electedcategory_id.

Pirates of the Caribbean 4 Rob Marshall 2011 1.

Forget Sarah Marshal Nicholas Stoller 2008 2.

WHERE the clause is combined with the keyword - IN

The WHERE clause, when used in conjunction with the IN keyword, only affects rows whose values match the list of benefits specified in the IN keyword. Help IN reduce the amount of OR clauses you may use.

The following query contains rows in which the number of members is 1, 2, or 3.

SELECTION * FROM `members` WHERE`

member_number` IN (1,2,3);

OR the clause is combined with - NOT IN Keyword.

The WHERE clause, used in conjunction with the NOT IN keyword, does not affect rows whose values match the list of values specified in the NOT IN keyword.

The following query contains rows whose subscription number is NOT 1, 2, or 3.

SELECTION * FROM `members` WHERE` member_number` NOT IN (1, 2, 3);

OR the clause is combined with - COMPARISON OF THE OPERATOR.

Comparison operators less than (), equal (=), non-similar (), can be used with the Where clause

= Equal.

The following script gets all female members of a member table using the peer comparison operator.

SELECTION * OF 'MEMBERS' OERE 'sex' = 'woman';

> More than.

The following script receives all payments higher than 2,000 from the payments table.

SELECTION * FROM `payment`

WHERE`paid_account`> 2000;

<> Not equal.

The following script gets all movies whose category ID is not 1.

SELECTION * FROM `movies` WHERE` category_id` <> 1;

The SQL WHERE clause limits the number of rows affected by a SELECT, UPDATE, or DELETE query.

The WHERE clause can be used in conjunction with logical operators such as AND and OR, comparison operators such as = etc.

When used with AND logical operators, all criteria must be effectively met.

When used with an OR logical operator, one of the criteria must be met.

The critical word IN is used to select the rows that correspond to the list of values.

The WHERE keyword is used to obtain filtered data in the result set.

O WH is the clause.

The WHERE clause is put-upon when you want to extract some data from a table, excluding other irrelevant data. E.g. when you want to display information about Grade 10 students only, you need information about Grade 2 students. Obtaining information about all students would increase query processing time.

Therefore, SQL provides a feature called the WHERE clause, which we can use to limit the extracted data. The condition that you specify in the WHERE clause filters the rows that are retrieved from the table and provides you with only the rows that you expected. The term WHERE can be used in conjunction with SELECT, DELETE, UPDATE.

Syntax of the SQL WHERE clause.

Where do you compare the value of the comparison operator?

The syntax of the WHERE clause with the Select statement is as follows:

SELECT LIST OF COLUMNS FROM NAME OF TABLE

Where is the condition;

Column or expression: is a column of a table or expression.

Comparison operator - operators like = <> etc.

Value: any user value or column name for comparison.

E.g., to find the name of a student with ID 100, the query will be:

CHOOSE name_name, name_name.

O id = 100;

Comparability operators and logical operators are used in the WHERE clause. These operators are discussed in the next section.

NOTE: Aliases defined for columns in a SELECT statement cannot be used in a WHERE clause to identify conditions. Only aliases made for tables can be used to call table columns.

How to use facial in the WHERE clause?

Facial can also be used in the WHERE clause of a SELECT clause.

For example, consider a table of employees. If you want to display the employee's name, current payroll, and a 20% increase only for products whose pay increment exceeds 30,000, then the SELECT statement can be written as follows.

SELECTION of names, salaries, wages * 1.2 AS new payment of employees.

Where he pays * 1, 2> 30000;

It is used to obtain data according to specific criteria.

The keyword WHERE can also be used to filter the data by correspondence.

Basic syntax:

CHOOSE COLUMN 1, COLUMN 2, FROM THE NAME OF THE TABLE, OR IS THE FUNCTIONAL VALUE OF THE COLUMN;

column1, column2: fields of the table.

Table name: The name of the table.

Column name: Name of the area used to filter the data.

Operator: Operation to take into account for filtering.

Value: The exact amount or model to obtain related data in the result.

The WHERE clause permits you to limit the result set to those that interest you.

In the last session, we used a SQL SELECT statement to recall all records from a database table. This is amazing if we want to see each file, but what happens if we are interested only in certain information? For example, what would happen if we were only interested in people whose names were Homer?

We could use the WHERE clause.

With WHERE, you can only filter records that satisfy the given condition.

In fact, in the previous lesson, we used the WHERE clause to select records in multiple tables. Here is a closer look at the WHERE clause.

Syntax SQL WHERE

SELECTION * OF FAME_name.

WHERE column name = 'criteria';

An example

SQL statement where

INDIVIDUAL SELECTION *

WHERE First Name = 'Homer';

Multiple conditions

You can filter records based on various shapes using the operator. Two known operators are AND and OR operators.

The And operator.

The AND operator filters the query only in records

satisfying the first and second conditions.

INDIVIDUAL SELECTION *

WHERE Given name = 'Homer.'

And Name = 'Brown';

The Or operator.

The OR operator filters the query only in records that satisfy either condition.

INDIVIDUAL SELECTION *

WHERE Given name = 'Homer.'

O Name = 'Ozzbourne';

CHAPTER FOUR

SQL joins using WHERE or ON

Filtered in the ON clause

Typically, filtering is handled in the WHERE clause once the two tables have already merged. You may want to filter one or both tables before entering them. For example, you only want to create table-to-table matches under certain circumstances.

Using the Crunchbase data, let's look at another LEFT JOIN example from the previous lesson (this time we'll add the ORDER BY clause):

SELECTION OF THE COMPANY. AS permanent link companies_permalink.

Companies. name AS company name.

Acquisitions.company_permalink AS

acquisitions_permalink.

Acquisitions.acquired_at AS acquired_date.

From a company tutorial.crunchbase_companies.

LEFT JOIN acquisitions tutorial.crunchbase_

IN   companies.permalink   =
acquisitions.company_permalink.

ORDER UP TO 1

Compare the following query to the previous query, and you will see that all the contents of the tutorial.crunchbase_acquisitions table are attached, except for the line for which company_permalink '/ company / 1000memories':

SELECTION OF THE COMPANY. AS permanent link companies_permalink.

Companies. name AS company name.

Acquisitions.company_permalink AS

acquisitions_permalink.

Acquisitions.acquired_at AS acquired_date.

From a company tutorial.crunchbase_companies.

LEFT JOIN acquisitions tutorial.crunchbase_

IN companies.permalink =

acquisitions.company_permalink.

Andacquire.company_permalink! = '/ Company /
1000memories'

ORDER UP TO 1

Filtered in the WHERE clause

If you move the same trickle to the WHERE clause, you will detect that the screen appears once the tables are attached. The result is that the 1000memories line is written to the original design, and then wholly filtered (in both tables) in the WHERE clause before the results are displayed.

SELECTION of companies. Permalink AS

companies_permalink.

Companies.name AS company name.

Acquisitions.company_permalink AS

acquisitions_permalink.

Acquisitions.acquired_at AS acquired_date.

From a company tutorial.crunchbase_companies.

LEFT JOIN acquisitions tutorial.crunchbase_

IN companies.permalink =

acquisitions.company_permalink.

WHERE acquisitions.company_permalink! = '/ Company / 1000memories'

Oracquisition.company_permalink IS NOT NULL.

ORDER UP TO 1

Refine your SQL skills

For this set of practical problems, we will introduce a new dataset: tutorial.crunchbase_investments. This table was also obtained from Crunchbase and contained much of the same information as the tutorial.crunchbase_companies Data. However, its structure is different: it contains one line per investment. There may be several investments in a company, and it is even possible that an investor could invest in the same company several times. Column names cannot be explained. The important thing is that company_ permalink from the tutorial .crunchbase_ investments and the table is given a permanent link in the tutorial. Crunchbase _companies Table. Note that some random information has been removed from this table because of this lesson

The syntax of the WHERE clause in SQL is as follows:

Where the conditions;

Parameters or arguments.

Terms

Conditions to be fulfilled for the selection of the recordings.

Example: a condition of the WHERE clause

The syntax of the SQL WHERE limitation is hard to explain. Let's start with a template that uses the WHERE clause to apply a single condition.

In this exercise, we have a table called providers with the following information:

Provider_idprovider_name city-state.

100 Microsoft Redmond, Washington.

200 Google Mountain View in California.

300 Oracle Redwood City, California.

400 Kimberly-Clark Irving, Texas.

500 Tyson Foods Springdale, Arkansas.

600 SC Johnson Racine, Wisconsin.

700 Dole Food Company, Village of Westlake, California.

800 Thomasville Georgia Food Flowers.

900 Electronic Arts Redwood City, California.

Enter the following SQL statement:

Try

SELECT *

FROM THE SUPPLIER

WHERE state = 'California';

Four records will be selected. Here are the results you should see:

Provider_idprovider_name city-state.

200 Google Mountain View in California.

300 Oracle Redwood City, California.

700 Dole Food Company, Village of Westlake, California.

900 Electronic Arts Redwood City, California.

In this example, we use the SQL WHERE clause to filter our results from the vendor table. The previous SQL statement would return all rows from the vendor table, where the state of California is located. Since * is used in the selection, all fields in the vendor table will appear in the results field.

Example: Two conditions in the WHERE clause (a condition I).

You can use the AND state of the WHERE clause to specify several requirements that must be met for the selected record. Let's see how to do that.

In this exercise, we have a table called Buyers that contains the following information:

CUSTOMER_ID last_namefirst_namefavorite_website.

4000 Jackson Joe techonthenet.com.

5000 Smith Jane digminecraft.com.

6000 Ferguson Samantha bigactivities.com.

7000 Reynolds Allen checkyourmath.com.

8000 Anderson Paige NULL.

9000 Johnson Derek techonthenet.com.

Now enter the following SQL statement:

Try

SELECT *

BUYERS

WHERE favorite_website = 'techonthenet.com'

And customer_id> 6000;

A record will be selected. Here are the results you should see:

CUSTOMER_ID last_namefirst_namefavorite_website.

9000 Johnson Derek techonthenet.com.

This example uses the WHERE clause to define multiple conditions. In this case, this SQL statement uses the AND clause to return all clients whose preferred website is techonthenet.com and whose client ID is greater than 6000.

Example: Two conditions in the WHERE clause (condition OR).

You can use the OR condition of the WHERE clause to test multiple situations in which a record is returned if one of the requirements is met.

In this example, we have a table named Products containing the following information:

product_idproduct_namecategory_name.

One pear 50

Two bananas 50

Three orange 50

Four blocks 50

5 75 bread

Six ham 25

7 NULL fabrics

Now enter the following SQL statement:

Try

SELECTION *

Of products

WHERE product_name = 'Pear'

Or product_name = 'Apple';

Two recordings will be selected. Here are the results you should see:

product_idproduct_namecategory_name.

One pear 50

Four blocks 50

This sample uses the WHERE clause to define multiple conditions, but instead of using the AND condition, use the OR condition. In this case, this SQL statement would return all records in the product table whose pear name is Pear or Apple.

Example: A combination of AND and OR conditions.

You can also combine the AND status with the OR condition in order to test more complex situations.

Let's use the product table again for this example.

product_idproduct_namecategory_name.

One pear 50

Two bananas 50

Three orange 50

Four blocks 50

Five bread 75

Six ham 25

7 Kleenex NULL

Now enter the following SQL statement:

Try

SELECTION *

Of products

WHERE (product_id> 3 AND category_id = 75)

OR (product_name = 'Pear');

Two recordings will be selected. Here are the results you should see:

product_idproduct_namecategory_name.

One pear 50

Five bread 75

CHAPTER FIVE

FROM in SQL

SQL clause: FROM

This SQL guide explains how to use the SQL FROM requirement with syntax and examples.

Description.

The SQL FROM clause is used to enumerate the tables and combinations needed for the SQL statement.

The syntax.

The syntax of the FROM clause in SQL is as follows:

From Table 1

[INSIDE JOIN

| LEFT [OUTSIDE] JOIN

| RIGHT [OUTSIDE] JOIN

| FULL [OUTER] JOIN} table2

ON table1.column1 = table2.column1]

Parameters or contentions

Table1 and table2

These are the tables utilised in the SQL statement. Both tables are joined according to table1.column1 = table2.column1.

When the FROM clause is used in an SQL statement, there must be at least one table specified in the FROM clause.

If two or more tables are listed in the SQL FROM clause, these tables are usually joined using an INNER or OUTER join.

Example: a table listed in the FROM clause

We will begin by considering how to use the FROM statement that contains a single table in an SQL statement.

In this sample, we have a table called providers with the following information:

provider_idprovider_name city-state.

100 Microsoft Redmond, Washington.

200 Google Mountain View in California.

300 Oracle Redwood City, California.

400 Kimberly-Clark Irving, Texas.

500 Tyson Foods Springdale, Arkansas.

600 SC Johnson Racine, Wisconsin.

700 Dole Food Company, Village of Westlake, California.

800 Thomasville Georgia Food Flowers.

900 Electronic Arts Redwood City, California.

Enter the following SQL statement:

SELECT *

FROM THE SUPPLIER

WHERE vendor_id<400

ORDER BY DESC city;

Three records will be selected. Here are the results you should see:

provider_idprovider_name city-state.

300 Oracle Redwood City, California.

100 Microsoft Redmond, Washington.

200 Google Mountain View in California.

In this example, we use the FROM clause to list a table called providers. There was no merge in this query because we only listed one table.

Example: Two tables in the FROM (INSIDE) clause.

Let's see how to use the RELATION clause. JOIN both tables together.

In this sample, we have a table called Products containing the following information:

product_idproduct_namecategory_name.

One pear 50

Two bananas 50

Three orange 50

Four blocks 50

5 75 bread

Six ham 25

7 NULL fabrics

And a table called categories containing the following information:

category_idcategory_name.

25 Deli

50 we produce

75 bakery

100 general merchandise

125 technology

Enter the following SQL statement:

SELECT products.product_name, groups.category_name.

OF PRODUCTS

INTERNAL CATEGORY

ON products.category_id = categories.category_id

O is the name of the product <> 'Pear';

Five records will be selected. Here are the results you should see:

product_namecategory_name.

Banana	products
Orange	product
Apple	product
bread	bakery

Sliced   ham

This example uses the FROM clause to merge two tables: products and categories. In this case, we use the OD clause to determine the INTERNAL UNION between product categories and tables based on the category_id column of both tables.

Example: Two tables of the FUT clause (OUTER JOIN).

Let's see how to use the FROM clause when we join two tables using OUTER JOIN. In this case, we will see the LEFT EXTERNAL CONNECTION.

We use the same product tables and categories from the previous example INNER JOIN, but this time we will join the tables using a LEFT OUTER JOIN. Enter the following SQL statement:

Try

SELECT products.product_name, groups.category_name.

OF PRODUCTS

LEFT EXTERIOR JOIN CATEGORIES

ON products.category_id = categories.category_id

O is the name of the product <> 'Pear';

Six records will be selected. Here are the results you should see:

product_namecategory_name.

Banana	products
Orange	product
Apple	product
bread	bakery
Sliced	ham
Null	fabric

The FROM clause can be simple and very intricate. However, in all cases, the critical point about the FROM clause is that it produces a tabular structure. This worksheet structure is known as the result set of the FROM clause. You can also see it as an intermediate result set, a standard result set, or an interstitial table. But regardless of whether the SELECT query retrieves data from a table, many tables, or other similar table structures, the result is always the same: The FROM statement generates a table structure.

Why start with the FROM clause?

To start writing a SELECT statement, my strategy is to omit the current SELECT clause and write the OD clause first. Finally, we will need to enter some expressions in the SELECT clause and use WHERE GROUP BY as well as other clauses. But there are good causes why we should always start with the OD clause:

If the FROM clause is incorrect, the SQL statement will always return false results. The FROM request generates a spreadsheet structure, an initial dataset in which all other operations are performed in a SELECT element.

The FROM clause is the first sentence that the database system observes when parsing an SQL statement.

Analyse the SQL statement

Whenever we send an SQL affirmation to the database for execution, the first action performed by the system is called analysis. This is how the database system tests the SQL statement to determine if there are any syntax errors. First, divide the report into its constituent clauses; then examine each clause based on the syntax rules for that clause. Contrary to what one might expect, the database system first parses the FROM clause instead of the SELECT statement.

For example, suppose we try to execute the following SQL statement in which, like computers, we have badly written computers:

SELECT

Username

OD

Theteans

Or

Conference = 'F'

In this case, the FROM clause brings up to a nonexistent table, so there is an immediate syntax error. If the database system first parsed the SELECT clause, it would be necessary to examine the table definitions of all tables in the database, looking for a definition that could contain two columns named name and ID. It is quite common for a database to have multiple two-column tables named name and ID. There could be confusion, and the database would require more information to know from which table to extract its name and identification. So, why the database system parses the FROM clause in the first place, and this is the first clause we are also thinking about.

Of the table

We have already seen the FROM clause with a single table. In Chapter 1, Introduction to SQL, we saw that the FROM clause specifies a team table:

SELECT

Username

OD

Hardware

In Chapter 2, Understanding the SELECT Command, we saw that the FROM clause specifies a table of entries:

SELECT

Title category

OD

Tickets

This kind of the FROM clause is as simple as it seems. There must be at least one specific table structure, and one table meets this requirement. When we want to return data from multiple tables at the same time; however, we should start by using combinations.

FROM more than one table using JOIN

An alliance connects, connects or combines two tables. The union starts with two tables, then combines or associates them in different ways, thereby creating a single spreadsheet structure (the result of the alliance). The verb "to join" is very descriptive of what is happening, as we will see in a moment.

Table Merge Method: The combination type is specified in the FROM clause using specific keywords, as well as the JOIN keyword. I will briefly describe different kinds of alliances to see how they differ. We will then see specific binding examples, using our application examples.

Types of compounds

The combination combines the rows of two tables according to a rule called the combination condition. This compares the row values in the two tables to determine the rows to join.

There are three basic types of merge:

Internal merge, created by the keywords INNER JOIN

External seal, which comes in three models:

LEFT OUT JOIN

RIGHT EXTERNAL COUNCIL

JOIN COMPLETELY

Cross-linking, created using CROSS JOIN keywords.

To visualise the operation of the merge, we will use two arrays called A and B, as shown below.

In Tables A and B.

These tables are too simplistic because they blur the difference between table and column names. The merge condition specifies the columns that must match. Also, it is not common for tables to have a single column.

Do not worry about what A and B might represent. They could be anything. The idea in the following illustrations is to focus your attention on the values of the lines that merge. Table A has a column called an attribute and rows with values 102, 104, 106, and 107. Table B has a column called by rows with values 101, 102, 104, 106, and 108.

Internal Union

Only personal lines that fulfil the ON element condition are returned for internal merge. Internal junctions are the most common types of terminals. In most cases, as in the example below, the ON clause specifies that both columns should have the appropriate values. In this case, if the value (column a) of one row of a table (A) is equal to the value (column b) of one row from another table (B), the merge condition is satisfied. And these lines are merged:

SELECT

a, b

IZ

INTERNAL PROGRAM B

EN a = b

As you can see, the line of A joins the line of B when their values are equal. Therefore, the values 102, 104, and 106 are returned in the result set. The value 107 in A does not match B and is therefore not included in the result set. Likewise, the values 101 and 108 in B do not compete with A and are therefore not included in the result set. If this is easier, you can think of it as matching lines in a long line, which then acts on the rest of the SELECT statement.

Joining abroad

Then we will see the outer joints. External mergers are different from internal alliances, in that mismatched rows can also be returned. As a result, most people say that the external union includes lines that do not fit the condition of the union. That's fine, but it could be a little misleading because foreign mergers add all the matching lines. Common external seals have many parallel lines, and only a few do.

Report an ad.

There are three types of external coupling: left, right and complete. We will start with the left external linkage.

Joining left outside.

For the left external union, all rows in the left table are returned, whether or not they have a corresponding row in the table on the right. What is the left table, and what is right? These are simply the tables mentioned on the left and right of the word OUTER JOIN. For example, in the next sentence, A is the left table and B is the right table, and the remaining outer combination is specified in the FROM clause:

SELECT

a, b

IZ

OUTSIDE LEFT JOIN B

EN a = b

The following image shows the results of this association. Remember: the left outer joins return all the rows in the left chart, as well as the corresponding lines in the right table if any.

Note that all values in point A are returned because A is a left table. In case 107, which did not correspond to B, we see that it is included in the results, but this set of results of B has no value. For the moment, it is correct to think that the value of B is missing, which of course, for 107 is.

Join on the right.

For the right outer join, all rows in the right table are returned regardless of whether they have a match in the left table. In other words, the right exterior combination acts exactly like the left exterior combination, except that all rows in the right table are returned:

SELECT

a, b

IZ

EXTERNAL RIGHTS JOIN B

EN a = b

In the previous example, A is still the left table and B is always the right table because the keywords OUTER JOIN are mentioned there. Therefore, the result of the merger contains all the rows in Table B, as well as the corresponding rows in Table A.

The right external articulation is opposite to the left external coupling. With the same tables in the same point, A as the left table and B as the correct table, the results of the right outer joint are very different from those of the left external union. This time, all B values were returned. In cases 101 and 108, which did not correspond to A, they are included in the results, but some lines do not indicate any value for some of the results A. Again. These A values are missing, but the line always returns.

A complete external union

For the entire foreign community, all rows in both tables are returned, whether or not they fit into another table. In other words, the full external combination works in the same way as the left and right outer combinations, except that all rows in both tables are returned this time. Consider this example:

SELECT

a, b

OD

JOIN COMPLETELY

EN a = b

Again, A is the table on the left, and B is the table on the right, although this time, it does not matter. The complete external links return all the rows of the two tables, as well as the corresponding rows of the second table, if any, as shown below.

The full outer suit is a combination of left and right upper garments. (Technically, if you remember the predetermined mathematical theory at school, you have to combine the results of the left and right external combination). The corresponding lines are of course, included, but tracks that do not match any table are added.

CHAPTER SIX

AND in SQL

A combination of AND and OR conditions.

This SQL tutorial explains how to use AND and the OR condition together in a single query with syntax and examples.

Description.

The AND and OR SQL statements can be combined to test multiple terms in a SELECT, INSERT, UPDATE, or DELETE comment.

When you combine these conditions, it is essential to use parentheses to tell the database in which order it can evaluate each situation. (Like when I learned the order of operations in math class!)

Syntax.

The syntax for the AND and OR states in SQL are as

follows:

O is the condition1

I condition2

Or state_n;

Parameters or arguments.

Condition1, condition2, ...condition_n.

Conditions being evaluated to determine if the records are selected.

Note

The AND & OR SQL conditions allow testing of several conditions.

Remember the order of the operating media!

Example: Using the "Y" and "O" Conditions with the SELECT Command.

Now, let's look at sample of using the AND condition and the OR state in a SELECT statement.

In this section, we have a table called Service Providers that contains the following information:

Provider_idprovider_name city-state.

100 Microsoft Redmond, Washington.

200 Google Mountain View in California.

300 Oracle Redwood City, California.

400 Kimberly-Clark Irving, Texas.

500 Tyson Foods Springdale, Arkansas.

600 SC Johnson Racine, Wisconsin.

700 Dole Food Company, Village of Westlake, California.

800 food flowers from Thomasville, Georgia.

900 Electronic Arts Redwood City, California.

Enter the following SQL statement:

SELECTION *

FROM the service provider

WHERE (state = 'California' AND provider_id<> 900)

OR (provider_id = 100);

Four records will be selected. Here are the results you should see:

Provider_idprovider_name city-state.

100 Microsoft Redmond, Washington.

200 Google Mountain View in California.

300 Oracle Redwood City, California.

700 Dole Food Company, Village of Westlake, California.

This example would return all vendors in the state of California, but does not have a vendor ID of 900. The query also returns all vendors with vendor IDs equal to 100. The brackets specify the vendor ID order in which the AND conditions are evaluated. And OR. Just as you learned in a series of mathematical operations!

Example: Using "Y" and "O" conditions with UPDATE statements.

Then, let's take a look at how the AND and OR terms are used in the UPDATE statement.

In this example, we have a table called clients that contains the following information:

website_idlast_namefirst_namefavorite_website.

4000 Jackson Joe techonthenet.com5000 Smith Jane digminecraft.com

6000 Ferguson Samantha bigactivities.com

7000 Reynolds Allen checkyourmath.com

8000 Anderson Paige NULL

9000 Johnson Derek techonthenet.com

We will now show how to use the AND and OR conditions to update the records in the table. Enter the following UPDATE statement:

Update your customers

SET favorite_website = 'techonthenet.com'

WHERE client_ID = 6000

OR (customer_id> 7000 and name <> 'Johnson');

There will be two records updated. Reselect the data in the user's table:

SELECTION * OF BUYERS;

Here are the results you should see:

website_idlast_namefirst_namefavorite_website.

4000 Jackson Joe techonthenet.com

5000 Smith Jane digminecraft.com

6000 Ferguson Samantha techonthenet.com

7000 Reynolds Allen checkyourmath.com

8000 Anderson Paige techonthenet.com

9000 Johnson Derek techonthenet.com

This example would update all the personal website values from the user's table to "techonthenet.com" where customer_id is 6000 and records where customer_id is greater than 7000 and where lastname_ is not equal at "Johnson." As you can see, the value of pages 3 and 5 have been updated.

Example: Using "Y" and "O" conditions with DELETE instructions.

Then, let's see how to combine the AND and OR terms to delete records using the DELETE statement.

In this example, we have a table called Products containing the following information:

Product_idproduct_namecategory_name.

One pear 50

Two bananas 50

Three orange 50

Four block 50

Five bread 75

Six ham 25

7 Kleenex NULL

Enter the following DELETE statement:

Delete products

OERE category_id = 25

O (product_id<4 and product name <> 'Banana');

Three records will be deleted. Select the information in the product table again:

PRODUCT SELECTION *;

Here are the results you should see:

Product_idproduct_namecategory_name.

Two bananas 50

Four block 50

5 75 bread

7 NULL fabrics

CHAPTER SEVEN

OR in Sql

SQL: or state.

This SQL guide explains how to use SQL OR land with syntax and examples.

Description.

The SQL OR clause allows you to test multiple conditions in the SELECT, INSERT, UPDATE, or DELETE commands. All requirements must be met for the selection of records.

The syntax.

The syntax for the OR state in SQL is as follows:

O is the condition1

Or condition2

Or state_n;

Parameters or arguments

Condition1, condition2, ...condition_n

Different test conditions for each record. Each condition can be fulfilled to be included in the result set.

Example: Using the "O" condition with the SELECT command.

Let's look at a sample that shows how to use an OR state in a SELECT command to test multiple situations in which any case must be met to select records.

In this example, we have a table named Service Providers that contains the following information:

Provider_idprovider_name city-state.

100 Microsoft Redmond, Washington.

200 Google Mountain View in California.

300 Oracle Redwood City, California.

400 Kimberly-Clark Irving, Texas.

500 Tyson Foods Springdale, Arkansas.

600 SC Johnson Racine, Wisconsin.

700 Dole Food Company, Village of Westlake, California.

800 food flowers from Thomasville, Georgia.

900 Electronic Arts Redwood City, California.

We will now show how to use the OR condition to test two conditions. Enter the following SELECT statement:

Try

SELECTION *

FROM the service provider

WHERE city = 'Mountain View'.

Or Supplier_id = 100

ORDER BY NAME OF SELLER;

Two recordings will be selected. Here are the results you should see:

Provider_idprovider_name city-state.

400 Google Mountain View in California.

100 Microsoft Redmond, Washington.

This example returns all providers located in the city of Mountain View or whose vendor ID is equal to 100. Since * is used in the SELECT statement, all fields in the vendor table are displayed in the result set.

Example: Using the "O" condition with the UPDATE

statement.

The OR condition can be used in the SQL UPDATE statement to test multiple concepts.

In this part, we have a table called clients that contains the following information:

website_idlast_namefirst_namefavorite_website.

4000 Jackson Joe techonthenet.com

5000 Smith Jane digminecraft.com

6000 Ferguson Samantha bigactivities.com

7000 Reynolds Allen checkyourmath.com

8000 Anderson Paige NULL

9000 Johnson Derek techonthenet.com

Enter the following UPDATE statement:

UPDATE YOUR CUSTOMERS

SET favorite_website = 'techonthenet.com'

WHERE client_ID = 5000

Or last_name = 'Reynolds'

Or first name = 'Paige';

There will be three updated records. Reselect the data in

the user's table:

SELECTION * OF BUYERS;

Here are the results you should see:

website_idlast_namefirst_namefavorite_website.

4000 Jackson Joe techonthenet.com

5000 Smith Jane techonthenet.com

6000 Ferguson Samantha bigactivities.com

7000 Reynolds Allen techonthenet.com

8000 Anderson Paige techonthenet.com

9000 Johnson Derek techonthenet.com

This example would update all personal site values in a user table on techonthenet.com where the user ID is 5000 or the Reynolds surname or Paige first name. As you can see, the favourite site field in the second, fourth, and fifth lines is updated.

Example: Using the "OR" condition with the DELETE statements.

Next, let's see how to use the OR condition in the DELETE statement to test all the requirements that must be met before deleting a record.

In this part, we have a table called Products containing the following information:

Product_idproduct_namecategory_name.

One pear 50

Two bananas 50

Three orange 50

Four blocks 50

Five bread 75

Six ham 25

7 Kleenex NULL

Enter the following DELETE statement:

Delete products

WHERE product_name = 'Pear'

Or product_name = 'Apple'

Or category_id = 25;

Three records will be deleted. Select the information in the product table again:

PRODUCT SELECTION *;

Here are the results you should see:

Product_idproduct_namecategory_name.

Two bananas 50

Three orange 50

5 75 bread

7 NULL fabrics

CHAPTER EIGHT

The difference between internal and external unions.

The results of the external combination will always be equal to the results of the corresponding internal mixture between the two arrays, plus the incompatible lines of the left panel, the right group, or both, depending on whether the mixture is left, right, or full.

Therefore, the difference between the left outer and the right external combination is simply the difference between the return lines in the left table with or without a match in the table on the right, or the next range of rows in the table of power with or without table ranks on the left.

Meanwhile, the complete outdoor combination always includes the results of the left and right outer combinations.

The cross joins

To join, each row of two tables assigned to each row of another table is returned, whether they match or not. The difference between cross unions is that it does not have an ON clause, which you can see in the following query:

SELECT

a, b

OD

BLOOD join B

The cross may be useful, but it is quite rare. Its purpose is to produce a spreadsheet structure containing rows that are representing all possible combinations of two sets of values (in our example, columns from two tables), as shown in Figure 3.6, "CROSS JOIN B"; This can be useful for generating test data or searching for missing values.

Old-fashioned unions

There is another type of combination which contains a comma-separated list of tables in the FROM clause with the combination conditions required in the WHERE clause; this type of combination is sometimes called a combination of "old-style," "comma list" or "WHERE clauses." For example, for tables A and B, it would look like this:

SELECT

a, b

OD

A B

O

a = b

These odd combinations can only be internal; other types of merge are possible only with a very exclusive and confusing syntax, which the same system manufacturers advise to use. Compare this to the recommended syntax for the internal binding:

SELECT

a, b

OD

INTERNAL UNION B

EN a = b

You can see these old unions in nature, but I warn you not to write them yourself. Always use the JOIN syntax.

There are three basic combinations and five different

variants to renew our team combination:

Join internally.

Left external union, right external union and complete external union.

The covenant of the cross.

Now for some more realistic examples.

The real world unites

In the second chapter, which contains a general description of the SELECT statement, we present a table of entries in the content management system that we will continue to use in subsequent queries to show how to write combinations, the "input table" shows some but not all of its content. For example, the content column is missing.

Within our CMS website, the goal is to give each category its area of the site, linked from the main menu and the leading site. The scientific field will contain all entries in the science category, the field of humour will provide all entries of the category humour and similar, as indicated in the "Proposed CMS Site Structure." For this purpose, each entry receives a note, stored in the category column of each line.

The main category pages require more than the name of

the word category we see in the input table. Visitors to the page would like to understand the content of each section. We will need a more descriptive name for each category. But where can it be stored on the site? We could code the longest name directly on each significant section of the website. However, a better solution would be to save the name in the database. The second table will work well. So we created a category table. We will give you two category columns and title, "Category Table."

The category column is the key for each row in the category table. This is called a key because the values in this column are unique and identify each row. This is the column we will use to join the list table.We'll learn more about keyboard design in Chapter 10; Relative Integrity. At this point, let's explore different ways to associate categories and lists of lists.

Create a category table.

The script used to create the category table is in Appendix C, Script Examples, and to download the book to a file named CMS_05_Categories_INNER_JOIN_Entries.sql.

Internal union: categories and entries

The first type of union that we will see is the internal union:

SELECT

Category .name, tickets. Title, tickets.created

OF

Category

INNER JOIN Tickets

IN entry.category = categories.category

The pursuing figure shows the results of this query.

Let's take a look at the query clause and look at what you do when we compare the query to the results it produces. The first part of the question to consider is, of course, the OD:

OF

Category

INNER JOIN Tickets

In the tickets. category = categories.category

The category table joins the list table with the INNER JOIN keywords. The ON clause specifies a union condition that indicates that the rows of two tables must match to participate in the union. Use dot notation (table name, line name) to indicate that the rows of a category table matches the rows of an input table only if the values of the columns in their category are the same. We will see in more detail the designation of the point in this chapter.

The image below shows in detail how to query a result set by internally merging a category table into an input table. Since this is an internal union, each row of a category table joins only rows in the input table that have the corresponding values in the relevant column columns.

Some of the entrance tables are hidden.

The list table has several additional columns that are not displayed: id, updated, and content. These columns are also available but omitted to simplify the diagram. The image would be rather messy if the content column were included because it contained several lines of text. Since these columns are not mentioned in the query, their inclusion in the diagram could be confusing. Some readers would inevitably ask, "Hey, where are they from?"

When it comes to matching category rows and listing tables, keep in mind that:

The line of the humour category corresponds to two-line entries, and in the results of the two cases, the path corresponds, and the name of the humour category appearing twice.

The blog category line does not match line entries. Therefore, since this is an internal alliance, this category does not appear in the results.

The rows of the other categories corresponded to a row of entries and these results corresponded.

By placing these observations in a slightly different way, we can see that a row in a category table cannot match any row, line, or more than one row in the input table.

The relationships

Several aspects of the relationship between a row in a category table and the corresponding rows in an input table are a fundamental feature of what we call a one-to-many relationship. Each category (one) can have several entries.

Although a specific category (blog) may not have appropriate entries and only one of the groups (humour) has multiple entries, but the relationship between classes and table entries still has a one-to-one structure. Once the tables are fully populated with real-time data, all types probably have multiple entries.

Looking at this relationship from another angle, so to speak, we can see that each entry can belong to a single category. This is a direct result of a category column in an input table that has a unique value that can match a single category value in the category table. However, many items may fall into the same category, as we have seen with humour entries. So the one-to-many relationship is also the one-to-many relationship. It only depends on the direction of the relationship being discussed.

Now that we have looked at the OD clause and see how it is located inside, and the ON condition has specified how tables should be joined, we can see the term SELECT:

SELECT

Categories .name, entries.title

, entries created

As expected, the SELECT clause specifies which columns of the result of the internal merge should be included in the result set.

Main notches

Note that the SELECT clause is now written line by column, using a convention called the first comma; this is used to separate the comma that's been used to separate the second and subsequent elements at the top of the line. It may seem new at first, but the syntax is right; Keep in mind that new paths and plain SQL are neglected, as is HTML. Experienced developers can get used to the end of comma-separated lines more easily, like this:

SELECT

catégories.nom,

tickets.title,

Created entries

I use commas as the encoding style convention to make SQL queries more readable and durable. The importance of readability and sustainability cannot be overstated. For example, see if you can notice two coding errors in this hypothetical query:

SELECT

Last name

The name

Title

The position,

Staff_id,

Group

Region

IZ

Staff

Now, see if you can notice the coding errors here:

Report an ad

SELECT

Last name

The nameTitle

Position

, scale_pay

Group

Region

,

IZ

Staff

A comma is missing in the query in the middle of the list, and there is an extra, unnecessary comma at the end of the list. In which example are the errors easier to detect?

Also, the first commas are more comfortable to manipulate if you modify your SQL code in a text editor using a keyboard. Sometimes, it is necessary to move or delete a column of the SELECT class, and it is easier to select (highlight) a line with the Shift and Arrow keyboards. Similarly, removing the last column also requires deleting the comma from the previous record, which is easy to forget. A comma entangled in front of the FROM keyword is a standard error that is difficult to resolve with the initial commas.

All columns are available after joining

With each combination, all columns in the associated tables are accessible for the SELECT query, even if the query does not use them. Let's take a look again at our internal connection:

SELECT

catégories.nom, entry. title, entries created

IZ

Categories

INNER JOIN Tickets

IN entry.category = categories.category

In most merge queries, merge tables typically contain more columns than those specified in the SELECT clause. This is also true here; the input table has other columns that are not specified in the query. "Internal Details" for the simplicity of the figure. Although the number is correct, it could be interpreted as a false misconception because it only shows the result of a set of queries, not a tabular structure produced by an internal merge.

The following figure shows the processing of the query and shows a tabular structure generated by the FROM clause and the internal union. It contains columns of two categories, one from each table. This worksheet, a long table, is produced by the database system at run time and is held temporarily for the SELECT clause.

When the union is executed in a query

Two essential points emerged from the analysis of our first example of union counselling:

The Union produces an intermediate set of results;

The SELECT clause comes after the FROM clause and run in the average result set.

At the beginning of this chapter, I pointed out that the FROM clause is the first clause parsed by the database system when we send a query. If there is no syntax error, the database system continues and runs the question. Well, it alternates out that the FROM clause is also the first clause to run the database system.

You can consider that the execution of a union query works as follows. First, the database system generates a set of standard Union-based tabular results specified in the FROM clause which contains all the columns of both tables. Then, the database system uses the SELECT statement to select only the specified columns from this intermediate result set and retrieve them from the final table structure returned as the result of the query.

Qualified column names

Finally, let's take a closer look at our internal combination query:

SELECT

categorías.nombre

, entry.title

, created tickets

OD

Categories

INNER JOIN Tickets

IN entry.category = categories.category

Each of the column names utilised in this query is qualified by the name of the table using a note point, and the name of the table preceding the name of the column with a space between them.

The qualification of the column name is required when there are multiple instances of the same column name in the query. (These would, of course, come from different tables, and numerous examples of the same column name in a single table are not possible because all columns in a table must have a unique name.) If you do not identify each column uniquely with the same name but are in different tables, the syntax for spelling mistakes. This applies whether the query refers to both columns or not; each reference must be qualified.

When there is only one instance of a column name in the query, the qualification of the column name becomes optional. Therefore, we could write the following and return to the same result set:

SELECT

Last name

Title

, created

OD

Categories

INNER JOIN Tickets

IN entry.category = categories.category

However, it is a good idea to evaluate all column names in this situation because when you examine the SELECT clause, you cannot always determine the table for each column. This can be especially frustrating if you know very little about the meals that are included in the board, for example when you solve a question written by another person (or even by you, a few months ago).

Always evaluate each column in the union query

Although some or all columns do not need to be assessed in a union query, and learning each column in a multi-table question is part of the correct SQL coding style because it is easy to understand.

In a way, the qualification of the column name automatically documents the request: the question is clearly defined, which facilitates the explanation in the documentation.

The nickname of the table

Another way to evaluate column names is to use alias tables. The nickname of the table is another name that is assigned to the table in the query. In practice, a table alias is usually shorter than the table name. For example, here is the same internal combination using a table alias:

SELECT

Nombre.cat

, ent.title

, Ent. created

OD

Categories like the cat

INNER JOIN AS Tickets

EN ent.category = cat.category

Here, a category table is assigned to the nickname and an alias ent is attached to the input table. You are free to choose the name that you want; the table names are temporary and are only valid during the consultation. Some people prefer to use simple letters as table aliases because   it reduces the number of characters in the query, which makes reading easier.

The only drawback to using a table alias is that once you

have assigned a table alias, you can no longer use the table name to evaluate your columns in that query and you must have a nickname consisting of the complete query. However, once the query is complete, you can return to the original table with your full name, the same alias, or even another nickname. The point here is that the alias table is defined only for the duration of the query that contains it.

Left external merge: categories and entries

Continuing with the search for combination queries, the left external merge query that we will look at is the same as the internal merge query we just described, except for the fact that it uses LEFT OUTER JOIN as a combination keyword:

SELECT

catégories.nom

, entry.title

, entries created

IZ

Categories

LEFT INPUT Join entries

IN entry.category = categories.category

The next figure shows the results of the previous query.

The only difference between this left outer combination query and the previous inner combination query is the inclusion of an extra row, for a category called Subscribe to My Blog in the result set. The second line is included because the query uses an external merge. In particular, it is a left external combination, and therefore all the rows in the left table and the category table, must be included in the results. Remember that the table on the left is simply the table mentioned to the left of the keywords LEFT OUTER JOIN.

To clarify which table is on the left and which table is on the right, we could write a merge without breaking the line and the spacing, so that the categories are more clearly the left table in this union:

From LEFT OUTSIDE JOIN classes.

Let's look at the results of the left external link because there is another important feature of the external links that I must clearly point out.

External connection request: site map

Looking at the answer of our LEFT OUTER JOIN query, it's easy to see how they could form the basis of a CMS site map. For example, the HTML code of a sitemap that can be obtained with these query results can be:

<h2>A few words of advice </ h2>

<Ul>

<li> Be the love of all (03/02/2009) </ li>

</ Ul

<h2> Stories of Identity </ h2>

<Ul>

<li> What happens if I get sick and die? (12/30/2008) </ li>

</ Ul

<h2> Subscribe to my blog </ h2>

<h2> Humorous anecdotes </ h2>

<Ul>

<li> Hello statue (2009-03-17) </ li>

<li> Uncle Karl and Gasoline (2009-02-28) </ li>

</ Ul

<h2>Our spectacular universe </ h2>

<Ul>

<li> Size of our galaxy (2009-04-03) </ li>

</ Ul

If you are a knowledge web developer, you can probably see how the results of the query will be converted to HTML using a specific application language.

Note that the category Join in my blog has no entry, but it is included in the result (because it is an external combination left). Therefore, the application logic should detect this situation and not create unordered list tags (<ul>) for entries in this category. Without going into the details of the programming logic of the application, I noticed that this has been done by detecting NULL in the input columns of this result line.

External connections are produced by NULL

Our left external union includes the left-hand table rows that do not match in the right-hand table, as shown in Figure 3.13, "Left external union results." What precisely are the values in the title and create columns for the blog results? Remember that these columns come from an input table.

The answer is: they are NULL.

NULL is a unique value in SQL that clearly represents the absence of a value. In the left outer combination, the columns from the right table for the incompatible rows in the left table are NULL in the result set. This means that there is no value here, which is logical because there is no corresponding line in the table on the right for this particular line in the left table.

Working with NULL is a part of everyday life when it comes to working with databases. We first found NULL (although briefly) in Chapter 1- Introduction to SQL, where it was used in the CREATE TABLE expression model, and we will see NULL again throughout the book.

Right External Alliance: Entries and Categories

The following right outer combo query gives the same results as the left combo query we just described:

SELECT

categorías.nombre

, entry.title

, created tickets

OD

Tickets

FOREIGN LAW JOIN CATEGORIES

IN entry.category = categories.category

But how can this be?

I hope you have seen the answer: I changed the order of the tables! In the right external query, I wrote:

FOREIGN RIGHT Tickets Join Categories.

In the previous external query, I had:

LEFT CONFERENCES VANJER Join the tickets.

The lesson to be learned from this deviation is simply that the left and right outer joins are precisely the same, it's just a matter of knowing which table will be outer: a table that will include all rows in the result set. As a result, many professionals avoid writing right external queries but convert them to left external unions by changing the order of the tables. Thus, the table from which all lines will always be returned is on the left. The remaining outer union seems to be much easier for most people than the right outer joints.

Right External Alliance: categories and entries

And what if the order of the tables of the other right outer combination had not changed? Suppose the query was:

SELECT

categorías.nombre

, entry.title

, created tickets

OD

Categories

FOREIGN LAW APPLY TO TICKETS

IN entry.category = categories.category

This time, as in the first left outer combination, the category table is on the left while the input table is on the right. The following figure shows that the results of this query are the same as those of the previous internal union.

How can this be? Is this more false? No, not this time. The reason is the actual content of the tables. Remember that the right outer join returns all the rows of the correct table with or without a match in the left table. The input table is the correct table, but in this case, each entry has a corresponding category. All entries are returned, and there are no incompatible lines.

Therefore, it is not wrong to show that the correct outer combination produces the same results as the inner combination because it has emphasised the rule for external combinations that all rows of an outer table returns with or without the corresponding lines if any. In this case, there was none.

To see the correct external combination in action, we need an entry with no matching category. Let's add a list to the worksheet for a new class called computers, as shown in the image below.

Test your SQL

An INSERT statement that adds this extra line to the input table is in the section titled "Content Management System."

"Combined External Query Results - Take-Two," shows that when we re-launched an actual external combined query with a new category, the results are the expected ones.

This time, we could see inconsistent entries in the query results because there are no rows in the computer category table.

Full external collaboration: categories and entries

Our next example of a union request is a completely external union. As you can predict, the overall syntax of combination queries is surprisingly similar to the other types of combinations that we have seen so far:

SELECT

catégories.nom

, entry.title

, tickets. created

IZ

Categories

JOIN COMPLETE ENTRIES

IN entry.category = categories.category

This time, the keywords of the union are FULL OUTER JOIN, but an unfortunate error occurs in at least one common database system. In MySQL, this does not support PUNI OUTER JOIN; although it is standard SQL, the result is the following syntax: SQL error: there is an error in SQL syntax; check in the manual corresponding to your MySQL server version that the correct syntax is used near "OUTER JOIN ON"

The following figure shows the result in other database systems that support PUNO OUTER JOIN.

Note that the result set includes incompatible rows from the left and right tables. This is a speciality full of exterior joints that we have seen before; both tables are external, so incomparable lines of both are also included. For this reason, complete external links are quite rare in Web development because many situations require them. On the contrary, left internal and external seals are quite common.

UNION asked

If your database system is not compatible with the FULL OUTER JOIN syntax, you can as well get the same results with a slightly more complex query called Union. Trade union consultations do not unite on their own. However, most people think of the results obtained by a union query consisting of two sets of merged or merged results. UNION requests only meet in a very lax sense.

Let's see a union query:

SELECT

catégories.nom

, entry.title

, tickets. created

IZ

Categories

LEFT INPUT Join entries

IN entry.category = categories.category

UNION

SELECT

catégories.nom

, entry.title

, tickets. created

IZ

Categories

RIGHT Join the tickets

IN entry.category = categories.category

As you can see, the left and right external queries we saw in this chapter are combined using the UNION keyword. The union query consists of multiple SELECT statements combined with a UNION operator. In this context, they are called sub queries because they are subordinates to the entire UNION query; they are only a part of the query, not that the query runs alone. Sometimes they are mentioned and approved, although this term is usually used to refer to a more specific situation with which we will soon become familiar with.

When properly executed, Operation UNION combines the result sets that's been generated by each of its sub selection queries into a result set. "How a Business Request Works" shows how it works in the previous example:

I mentioned earlier that a merge operation could be thought of as merging one row of a table at the end of a row in another table, a horizontal merge if you wish to call it. The join is like a vertical link: a second result set is added at the end of the first result set.

An exciting feature is that duplicates are deleted. You can see the clones quite quickly: they are whole lines where the value of each column is identical. The reason for creating copies in this example is because the two sub-selectors - left outer and right outer combinations - return rows from the same two tables that correspond to the same combination conditions. Therefore, the corresponding lines support both sub-selections, thus creating double lines in the mutual results. Only incompatible lines are not duplicated.

You may be wondering why UNION eliminates duplicates; the answer is simply that it is designed and that the work of a UNION operator should work.

UNION and UNION ALL

Sometimes, it is crucial to keep all the lines created by the merge operation and not to delete the duplicates. To do this, use the keywords UNION ALL instead of UNION.

UNION deletes duplicate rows. Only one row in each set of double rows is included in the result set.

UNION ALL keeps all the lines produced in the subdivisions of the Union, thereby maintaining the double lines.

UNION ALL is much faster because the dire need to look for duplicates to eliminate them is redundant.

The fact that our union query has deleted the duplicate rows means that the previous union query produces the same results as a full external union. Of course, this example is designed to do just that.

There is more to say about union queries, but for now, let's finish this section with one point: union queries, like union queries, produce a tabular structure; as a result, set.

Viewpoints

A view is another type of database aim that we can create, such as a table. However, opinions are not significant because they do not store data (unlike tables). Opinions are SELECT statements (often complex) that have been named for easy reference and reuse, and can be used for many purposes:

You can customise a SELECT statement by providing column aliases.

They can be a nickname for a result set that in its definition generated a SELECT statement. If the SELECT report in the view contains unions between multiple tables, then the database has already attached them before the query in the view. After All this query, then, is a table to consult. This is probably the most crucial benefit of using sight.

They can impose security on the database. Database users may have restrictions on the full display of the underlying tables; instead, they can only have access to the views. A classic example is a table of employees that contains columns such as name, department, and salary. Due to the confidential nature of wages, very few people were allowed to access this table directly; instead, a unique view is available that excludes the classified columns.

To illustrate this, here's how you define an internal combination query that was previously used as a view:

SELECT

categorías.nombre

, entry.title

, created tickets

OD

Categories

LEFT OUTSIDE JOIN THE TICKETS

IN entry.category = categories.category

UNION

SELECT

categorías.nombre, entry.title

, created tickets

OD

Categories

FOREIGN LAW APPLY TO TICKETS

IN entry.category = categories.category

Of course, this is not a table: the view itself does not

store the result set generated by its SELECT command. Using a view name here works by executing the underlying SELECT view statement, thereby storing its results in an intermediate table and using that table following the FROM clause. The results of the previous query, as shown below.

This result set is similar to that which is obtained by an internal union query, which defines the view. Note that only two columns have been returned because the SELECT element using light in the FROM clause (unlike the SELECT statement outlining the aspect) requires only two columns. Also, note that the alias in the Category Name column is assigned to the Name column of the category table in the view definition. This is the name of the column to use in any SELECT statement that uses the view, which is the name of the column used in the result set.

A specific implication of the view definition is that for each query that uses the view, only the columns that are defined in the SELECT view element are available. Although the input table contains a content column, and this view column is unknown and will generate a syntax error if a reference is used at the prompt.

Web development impressions

How do the aspects relate to our daily tasks as web developers?

When working on a large project in a team environment, you can only grant access to the views, and not to the underlying tables. For example, a database administrator (DBA) may have created a database, and you use it. You may not even clear the fact that you are using views. Indeed, syntactically, tables and figures are used in the FROM clause in the same way.

When creating a database, you can create views for convenience. For example, if you often need to display a list of ads and their categories are on different pages of a site, it is much easier to write OD_con_category entries than the next union.

Support derived tables too

We begin this chapter by examining the FROM clause, moving from simple tables to different types of combinations. We have briefly seen the UNION query and its sub-selections, as well as how the views facilitate the use of associated complex expressions. To finish this chapter, we will quickly see the derived tables. Here is an example:

SELECT

Title

, category name

IZ

(SELECT

tickets.title

, entries created

, groups.name AS category_name

IZ

Tickets

INTERNAL CATEGORY

IN category.category = entry.category

) AS entry_with_category

The table presented here represents the complete SELECT query in parentheses (the syntax is mandatory in parentheses to determine the attached query). A derived table is a mutual type of sub query, which is a subordinate or nested query in another query (similar to subsections of the union record).

And that sounds familiar. This request is the same as the one used in the entry_with_categories view defined in the previous section. Since each image needs a name, each derived table must also receive a name, even using the AS keyword (in the last line) to assign entry_with_category as the alias of the table to the derived table. Given these similarities, derived tables are often called standard views. In other words, they define a tabular structure, a set of results produced by a sub query, directly in (or in) SQL statements, and the tabular structure constructed by the sub query is used in turn as a data source for the clause. OD of external or primary consultation.

In summary, anything that produces a spreadsheet structure can also be specified as a data source in the FROM clause. Even the UNION query, described briefly, can also be used in a FROM requirement if it is defined as a derived table; the entire UNION query enters parentheses that limits the derived table.

Derived tables are incredibly useful in SQL. We will see some of them throughout the book.

Final: of the disposition.

In this section, we examine the FROM clause and how it determines the data source for a SELECT statement. There are many types of worksheets that can be specified in a FROM clause:

Individual tables

Associated tables

Comments

Support or derived tables

Finally, this is one of the critical concepts of the book, the FROM clause specifies not only one or more tabular structures from which data can be extracted, but the result of executing the FROM clause is another structure. Tabular, called average result score, or in the middle of the table. Typically, this intermediate table is created first, before the database system processes the SELECT clause.

The WHERE clause, we'll see how the WHERE clause can be used to filter the table structure produced by the FROM clause.

Join and Union can be used to combine data from one or more tables. The difference lies in the way the data is mixed.

In simple terms, combinations combine data in new columns. If two tables are joined, the data from the first table is displayed in a set of columns next to the column of the second table in the same row.

Unions combine data in new lines. If two tables are "joined" then the data in the first table is aligned while the data in the second table is in the second set. The lines are under the same result.

Each row of results contains the TWO columns of Tables A and B. Lines are created when the columns of one table correspond to the columns of another. This coincidence is called the condition of union.

It is ideal for searching for values and including them in the results. This is usually the result of denormalisation (deletion of normalisation), and involves the use of a foreign key in one table to search for column values using a primary key in another.

Now compare the description above with that of the alliance. In the community, each line appears in the results of one table O on another. In the city, the columns are not combined to create effects, and on the other hand the rows are connected.

Joints are typically used when you have two results whose rows you want to include in the same result. The use case can have two tables: teachers and students. You want to create a master list of names and birthdays sorted by date.

To do this, you can first use an alliance to combine the rows into a result, and then sort them.

Let's take a closer look at both.

Data combination with union.

In this section, we will see the inner union. This is one of the most common forms of aggregation. It is used when you have to align the rows of two tables. The parallel lines remain in the result, and they are the ones that are not ignored.

The following is an example of a simple select statement with an INNER JOIN clause.

SELECT column list

Of sustainable

INTERNAL JOIN

ON the common state of the second table.

Here is an example of using a combination to search for an employee's name:

SELECT Employee.NationalIDNumber,

Name of the person,

Person.LastName,

Employee.JobTitle

Human resources. employee

INTERNAL JOIN

Person person

ON HumanResources.EEmployee.BusinessEntityID = Person.BusinessEntityID.

ORDER BY PERSON. Last name;

You can get more information on INTERNAL ASSOCIATIONS here, but for now, I want to point out two things.

First, examine the state of the join and see how we associate the BusinessEntityID of the two tables.

Second, make sure that the results appear in the columns of both tables.

Data combination with UNION

Let's take a nearer look at the UNION statement. In SQL, the UNION statement looks like

SELECT column list

OF tables1

UNION

SELECT column list

OF tables2

Suppose that you are prompted to list all

AdventureWorks2012 product categories and subcategories. To do this, you can write two separate queries and provide two different results, such as two worksheets, or you can use the UNION clause to get results.

SELECTION C. Name

DE Manufacturing.Category of products as C

UNION ALL

SELECTION S.Name

DE Manufacturing.ProductSubcategory AS S

To join the two tables, there are several requirements:

The number of columns must be the same for both selected expressions.

The columns, regularly, must be of the same type of data.

When the lines are combined, the duplicates are then deleted. If you want to keep all rows of the results of the select statement, use the ALL keyword.

Union

The Union operator includes the results of two or more queries into a single, and independent result set that includes all rows belonging to all Union queries. In this operation, two more queries are combined, and the duplicates are deleted.

The SQL equivalent of the above information is provided below.

(

1 ID SELECTION

UNION

SELECTION 2

UNION

SELECTION 3

)

UNION

(

SELECTION 3

UNION

SELECTION 4

UNION

SELECTION 5

)

In the output, you can see a different list of records in both result sets.

Union all

When we look at the union against each other, we find that they are quite similar, but have significant differences from the results of the work.

The Union operator dwell the results of two or more queries into a result set that includes all rows belonging to all Union queries. In other words, combine two or more sets of lines and contain the duplicates.

The SQL equivalent of the above information is provided below.

(

1 ID SELECTION

UNION

SELECTION 2

UNION

SELECTION 3

)

UNION ALL

(

SELECTION 3

UNION

SELECTION 4

UNION

SELECTION 5

To cross

The interest operator keeps the lines common to all inquiries.

SQL view of previous tables

(

1 ID SELECTION

UNION

SELECTION 2

UNION

SELECTION 3

)

to cross

(

SELECTION 3

UNION

SELECTION 4

UNION

SELECTION 5

)

The SQL view of previous tables with the EXCEPT statement is provided below.

(

SELECTION 1 [missing only]

UNION

SELECTION 2

UNION

SELECTION 3

)

EXCEPT

(

SELECTION 3 B

UNION

SELECTION 4

UNION

SELECTION 5

)

It is easy to visualise an ensemble operator using a Venn diagram, where the intersection shapes represent each of the tables. The intersections of how the planes overlap are the lines in which the condition is fulfilled.

Syntax:

Syntax for Union and Union All SQL statements are as follows:

SELECTION Column1, Column2, ...ColumnN

DE <table>

[O conditions]

[GROUP BY Column (s)]

[Have terms]

UNION

SELECTION Column1, Column2, ...ColumnN

Of the table

[WHERE conditions);

ORDER Column1, Column2 ...

Rules:

Several rules apply to all established operators:

Explanation in each row or the number of columns defined in each query must have the same line.

The following sets of SQL statement strings must match the data type of the first query.

Square brackets can create other set operators in the same declaration.

It is possible to have the command ORDER BY, but it should be the last SQL statement.

BY and HAVING group restrictions can be applied to a single request.

Note:

All of these set operators eliminate duplicates except Union, and All.

The names of the output columns of the first query have been referred to, i.e. when we execute SELECT statements with one of the Set comments and the result set for each question can have names of the different column, and then the result of the command. The SELECT statement refers to the column names of the first query in operation.

SQL JOIN is most often used to combine columns from multiple linked tables, whereas SET operators combine rows from multiple tables.

When expression types are equal but differ in accuracy, scale, and length, the result is determined by the same expression combining rules.

Examples:

The following T-SQL queries are prepared and started in the Adventureworks2014 database. You can download a sample from the AdventireWorks2014 database here.

How to use a simple SQL Union clause when selecting a declaration?

In this example, the result set includes a set of lines separate from the first and second sets. The following example is based on rules 1, 3, and 5.

SELECTION *

OD

(

(

SELECTION 1 A

UNION

SELECTION 2

UNION

SELECTION 3

)

UNION

(

SELECTION 3 B

UNION

SELECTION 4

UNION

SELECTION 5

)

UNION ALL

(

SELECTION 8 c

UNION

SELECTION 9

UNION

SELECTION 1

)

) T;

How to use SQL Union with queries that have a WHERE clause

The following example shows that the use of the union in two SELECT clauses with WHERE and ORDER BY terms clauses.

The following example is based on rules 1, 2, and 3.

SELECTION P1.ProductModelID,

P1.Nombre

DE Production.ProductModel P1

O IS THE PRODUCTMODELID IN (3, 4)

UNION

SELECTION P2.ProductModelID,

P2.Nombre

DE Manufacturing.ProductModel P2

WHERE P2.ProductModelID IN (3, 4)

ORDER BY P1.Name;

The union adheres without union clause.

UNION STYLES

In simple terms, let's compare two styles of table combinations using SQL syntax and SAS® data steps. In a wise column, merge the two columns 'acol', and 'bcol' return with the result of a set as large as the intersection of tables a and b are attached

using the values of its standard 'key' key variable.

SELECTION a.col as acol, data _null_;

b.col as bcol fusion b;

DE by key;

Internal union b EN a.key = b.key run;

ACOL BCOL KEY

p one six

q two seven

r three eight

The combination of rows returns a single 'col' column instead of a result set containing all the rows of the constituent tables a and

b, regardless of the values in the "key" column of each table.

SELECT a column of _null_ data;

UNION establishes b;

SELECTION B-neck run;

Column

a

Two

Three

Six

Seven

Eight

The ambiguity about whether the aob table should be listed first before the UNION statement is an excellent clue for this query to be supported in the database. When consistent table sizes are small, query performance may not be noticeable.

However, when UNION members are involved in a complete selection of multiple tables or with the massive size of the content line executed by UNION,

then the query may not work but returns a terrible execution error 'Timeout time'.

Basic rules for combining two or more queries using UNION

Basic rules for combining two or more consultations with UNION:

1.) Multiple columns and column order of all queries must be the same.

2.) The data types of the table included in each request must be identical or compatible.

3.) Generally, column return names are extracted from the first query.

UNION acts by default as UNION [DISTINCT], i.e. deletes duplicate rows. However, using ALL-UNION keywords returns all lines, including duplicates.

Difference between SQL JOIN and UNION

1.) The columns of the union tables may be different in JOIN, but in UNION, the number of columns and the column order of all the queries must be the same.

2.) UNION defines the query lines one after the other (vertically), but JOIN defines the query column one after the other (defines horizontally). That is to say that it creates a Cartesian product.

Syntax:

SELECT <list_columns> t [INTO]

[O]

[GROUPS TO] [BEDS]

[UNION [ALL]

SELECTION <list_columns>

[O]

[GROUPS TO] [PAYMENT] ...]

[ORDER BY]

All queries are executed independently, but their output is connected.

In the following example, no clause with UNION has been added. As a result, UNION defaults to UNION [DISTINCT] and only single lines are available in the result set.

Sample table: Product.

PROD_CODE PROD_NAME COM_NAME LIFE

PR001 T.B. SONY 7

PR002 DVD PLAYER LG 9

PR003 IPOD PHILIPS 9

PR004 SONY 8 SON SYSTEM

PR005 MOBILE NOKIA 6

Example of a table: purchase

PUR_NO PROD_CODE PROD_NAME COM_NAME PUR_QTY PUR_AMOUNT

----

2 PR001 T.B. SONY 15 450000

1 PR003 IPOD PHILIPS 20 60000

3 PR007 LAPTOP COMPUTER H.P. 6 240000

4 PR005 MOBILE NOKIA 100 300000

5 DVD PLAYER PR002 LG 10 30000

6 PR006 CREATIVE SOUND SYSTEM 8 40000

SQL code:

SELECTION_product_products, product names

Product

UNION

SELECTION_product_products, product names

About the purchase;

a copy

Exit:

PROD_CODE PROD_NAME

PR001 T.B.

PR002 DVD PLAYER

PR003 IPOD

PR004 SON SYSTEM

PR005 MOBILE

PR006 SOUND SYSTEM

PR007 LAPTOP COMPUTER

SQL UNION ALL

In the following sample, the optional clause ALL is added to UNION for which all rows of each query are available in the result of the set. Here, in the previous output, the highlighted lines are not unique but are displayed. If ALL clauses are ignored, the highlighted lines appear once.

SQL code:

SELECTION PRO_code, add_name, com_name

Of the product

UNION ALL

SELECTION PRO_code, add_name, com_name

Buying;

SQL UNION ALL using where

In the following example, two queries were made using two different criteria, including the WHERE clause. As a result, all recovery lines (including duplicates) are displayed in the result set. In this example, the highlighted lines are the same, but this is indicated for the ALL clause with UNION. If ALL requests are ignored, then the label queues will appear once.

SQL code:

SELECTION PRO_code, add_name, com_name

OF PRODUCTS

O life> 6

UNION ALL

SELECTION PRO_code, add_name, com_name

PURCHASE

O pur_qty> 10

SQL UNION table by itself

In the following example, two queries were made using two different criteria for the same table. This shows all recovered lines (including duplicates). In this example, the highlighted lines are the same, but this is clearly indicated for the ALL clause with UNION.

SQL code:

SELECTION PRO_code, add_name, com_name

PURCHASE

O pur_qty> 6

UNION ALL

SELECTION PRO_code, add_name, com_name

PURCHASE

WHERE pur_amount> 100,000

SQL UNION with different column names

In the following Sample, two queries were made using two different criteria and different columns. The various columns in both statements are 'life' and 'pur_qty'. However, since the data types are the same for both columns, the result is displayed. The names of the returned columns are extracted from the first query.

SQL code:

SELECT product_code, add_name, life

OF PRODUCTS

O life> 6

UNION

SELECT product_code, add_name, pur_qty

PURCHASE

O pur_qty<20

SQL UNION with internal union

In the following example, the union is performed with two queries. The consultations are two internal statements of association. In the first query, the union is played between two tables in which the prod_ code of the two tables is very identical. In the second query, the union is performed between two tables in which the name_prod of the two tables is also very identical.

SQL code:

SELECT product.prod_code, product.product_name,

buy.pur_qty, buy.pur_amount

OF PRODUCTS

Buy INNER JOIN

ON product.prod_code = acquire.prod_code

UNION

SELECT product.prod_code, product.product_name,

buy.pur_qty, buy.pur_amount

Of the product

Buy INNER JOIN

ON produces.product_name = acquire.product_name;

SQL: Union against Union of all

The main difference between UNION and UNION ALL is that UNION deletes duplicate records, unlike UNION ALL. Apply these two commands to both tables1 and table2.

Rows in Table 1:

field1

1

4

2

3

Rows in Table 2:

field1

2

4

2

1

UNION example (delete all duplicate records):

SQL code:

SELECT case 1

From Table 1

UNION

SELECT claim 1

From the table2;

Copy

Exit:

field1

1

2

3

4

UNION ALL Example:

SQL code:

SELECT case 1

From Table 1

UNION ALL

SELECT claim 1

From the table2;

Copy

Exit:

field1

1

4

2

3

2

4

2

1

How to utilise the SELECT INTO clause and SQL Union

The following sample creates a new dbo.dummy table by using the INTO clause of the first SELECT statement, which contains the last result set Union of ProductModel columns and the name of two different result sets. In this case, it is generated from the same table, but in the real world, it can be two different tables altogether. The following example is based on rules 1, 2, and 4.

DROP TABLE IF dbo.dummy exists;

SELECTION P1.ProductModelID,

P1.Nombre

In the doll

DE Production.ProductModel P1

O IS THE PRODUCTMODELID IN (3, 4)

UNION

SELECTION P2.ProductModelID,

P2.Nombre

DE Manufacturing.ProductModel P2

WHERE P2.ProductModelID IN (3, 4)

ORDER BY P1.Name;

IR

SELECTION *

OD dbo.Dummy;

How to use SQL Union with WHERE and ORDER BY queries.

This is only possible if we use TOP functions or aggregation functions in the instructions of each operator in the selected Union. In this case, the first ten rows of each result set are listed and combined using the Union clause to get the final result. You will also see that the order by clause is placed in all selection declarations.

SELECTION a.ModelID,

Last name

OD

(

SELECTING THE TOP 10 PRODUCTSModelIDModelID,

Last name

DE Manufacturing.ProductModel

OR THE PRODUCT MODEL IS NOT IN (3, 4)

Sort by DESC

) a

UNION

SELECTION b.ProductModelID,

b. Last name

OD

(

SELECTION OF TOP 10 ProductModelID,

Last name

DE Manufacturing.ProductModel

O IS THE PRODUCTMODELID IN (5, 6)

Sort by DESC

) b;

How to use SQL Union and SQL Pivot

In the following example, we try to combine several results. In the real case, you can have financial figures from several regions or departments, and the tables can have the same columns and data types, but you may want to place them in a set of rows and a single report. In such a scenario, I would use a Union clause, and it would be easy to combine the results and convert the data into a more meaningful report.

In this Sample, ProductModel is classified as Top10, Top100, Top 100, and converts the rows into an aggregated set of values in the corresponding columns. The following example is based on rule 2.

MAXIMUM SELECTION (Top10) Top10,

MAX (Top100) Top100,

MAX (Top1000) Top100

OD

(

ACCOUNT SELECTION (*) Top10,

0 Top100,

0 Top1000

DE Manufacturing.ProductModel

WHERE ProductModelID<10

UNION

SELECTION 0,

```
COUNT (*),

0 0

DE Manufacturing.ProductModel

WHERE ProductModelID> 11

And ProductModelID<100

UNION

SELECTION 0,

0

COUNT (*)

DE Manufacturing.ProductModel

WHERE ProductModelID> 101

) T;
```

NULL values are fundamental for definition operators and are treated as second-class database citizens because NULL values are considered unique, and if two rows have NULL values in the same column, they will be regarded as identical. In this case, you compare NULL with NULL, and you get a tie. In the following sample, you will see the use of NULL values. In this case, it works with the aggregation function, max.

MAXIMUM SELECTION (Top10) Top10,

MAX (Top100) Top100,

MAX (Top1000) Top100

IZ

(

SELECTION ACCOUNT (*) Top10,

NULL Top100,

NULL Top1000

Production Product Model

WHERE ProductModelID<10

UNION

SELECT NULL,

ACCOUNT (*)

NULL

Production Product Model

WHERE ProductModelID> 11

And ProductModelID<100

UNION

SELECT NULL,

NULL

ACCOUNT (*)

Production Product Model

WHERE ProductModelID> 101

) T;

How to utilise SQL Union with group and property clauses:

The following examples use a union operator to combine the results of a table for which all conditional clauses are defined using the Group by and Have expression.

The last name is broken down by specifying the conditions in the clause that you have.

The following sample is based on rule 5.

SELECTION pp. Last name,

COUNT (*) repeated,

0 repeat three times

FROM.Person AS pp

JOIN HumanResources.E Employee AS and ON e.BusinessEntityID = pp.BusinessEntityID

GROUP BY pp.lastname

COUNT (*) = 2

UNION

SELECTION pp. Last name,

0

COUNT (*) NtoZRange

FROM.Person AS pp

JOIN HumanResources.E Employee AS and ON e.BusinessEntityID = pp.BusinessEntityID

GROUP BY pp. Last name

THIS NUMBER (*)> 2;

UNION deletes duplicate rows.

UNION ALL does not delete double lines.

Syntax

The syntax of the UNION manipulator in SQL is as follows:

SELECT expression1, expression2, ...expression_n

OF tables

[O conditions]

UNION

SELECT expression1, expression2, ...expression_n

OF tables

[WHERE conditions];

Parameters or arguments

expression1, expression2, expression_n

The columns or budgets that you want to resend.

Tables

Tables from which to extract records. There must be leastways for one table listed in the FROM clause.

Where are the conditions?

Optional. Conditions to be fulfilled for the selection of the recordings.

Note

There must be the same number of expressions in both SELECT expressions.

The corresponding expressions must have the same type of data in the SELECT elements. For example, expression1 must be of the same data type in the first and second SELECT statements.

See also UNION ALL operator.

Example: A field with the same name.

Let's see how to use the SQL UNION operator to return a field. In this simple sample, the field in both SELECT statements will have the same name and type of data.

For example:

SELECT provider_id

FROM the service provider

UNION

SELECT provider_id

OF commands

ORDER BY Vendor_id;

In this example, the UNION SQL statements, if vendor_id appears in the Providers and Orders table, then it will appear once in the result set. The UNION operator deletes duplicates. If you do not want to remove copies, try using the UNION ALL operator.

Now, let's explore this example in detail.

If you have filled the vendor table with the following records:

supplier_idsupplier_provider

1000 Microsoft

2000 Oracle

3000 apples

4000 Samsung

And the command table is populated with the following records:

order_idorder_datevendor_id

1 2015-08-01 2000

2 2015-08-01 6000

3 2015-08-02 7000

4 2015-08-03 8000

And he made the following UNION statement:

SELECT provider_id

FROM the service provider

UNION

SELECT provider_id

OF commands

ORDER BY Vendor_id;

You will get the following results:

Vendor identification

1000

2000

3000

4000

6000

7000

8000

As you can see in this example, UNION retrieved all vendor_id values from the vendor and order tables and returned a combined result set. Because the UNION operator has eliminated duplicates between result sets, 2000_ vendor_id only appears once, even though it is in both the vendor table and the ordering table. If you do not want to delete duplicates, try using the UNION ALL operator instead.

Example: different field names

The corresponding columns of each SELECT command do not need to have the same name but must have the same relevant data types.

When you do not have the same column names between SELECT statements, it becomes a little complicated, especially when you want to sort the results of a query using the ORDER BY clause.

Let's see how to use a UNION operator with different column names and sort the results of the query.

For example:

SELECT provider_id, provider name.

FROM the service provider

WHERE donor_id> 2000

UNION

CHOOSE the name of the company, the name of the company.

OF companies

WHERE company_id> 1000

ORDER UP TO 1;

In this example of SQL UNION, since the column names differ between the two SELECT statements, it is best to refer to the columns of the ORDER BY clause because of its position in the result set. In this example, we have sorted the results by vendor_id / company_id in ascending order, as shown in ORDER 1. The Supplier_id / company_id fields are in position 1 in the result set.

Now, let's explore this example with the data.

If you have filled the vendor table with the following records:

supplier_idsupplier_provider

1000 Microsoft

2000 Oracle

3000 apples

4000 Samsung

And the table of society is filled with the following records:

company_id Company name

1000 Microsoft

3000 apples

Sony 7000

8000 IBM

And you made the following statement from UNION:

SELECT vendor_id, vendor name

FROM THE SUPPLIER

WHERE vendor_id> 2000

UNION

CHOOSE the name of the company, the name of the company.

Enterprises

WHERE company_id> 1000

ORDER UP TO 1;

You will get the following results:

supplier_idsupplier_provider

3000 apples

4000 Samsung

Sony 7000

8000 IBM

First, note that the Supplier_id record of 3000 appears only once in the result set because the UNION query has deleted duplicate entries.

Second, keep in mind that the column headers in the result set are called vendor_id and the provider name. This is because of the column names used in the first SELECT statement in UNION.

If you wanted, you could have deleted the columns as follows:

SELECT provider_ID AS ID_Value, provider name AS Name_Value

FROM THE SUPPLIER

WHERE vendor_id> 2000

UNION

SELECT Company_ID AS ID_Value, Company Name AS Name_Value

Enterprises

WHERE company_id> 1000

ORDER UP TO 1;

From now on, the column headings of the result will be alienated as ID_Value for the first column and Name_Value for the second column.

ID_VALUE NAME_VALUE

3000 apples

4000 Samsung

Sony 7000

8000 IBM

Frequently asked Questions.

Question: I have to compare the two dates and return the

field number according to the value of the date. For example, the table refers to the last update date, and the field contains the date. I need to check if trunc (last_update_date> = trunc (sysdate-13).

Answer: As you use the COUNT function, which is an aggregate function, we recommend that you use Oracle UNION. For example, you can try the following:

SELECT the code AS a.code, a.name Name AS, COUNT (b.Ncode)

OD cdmaster a, nmmaster b

O a.code = b.code

And a.status = 1

And b.status = 1

And b.Ncode<> 'a10'

I TRUNC (last_update_date) <= TRUNC (sysdate-13)

GROUP BY a.code, a.name

UNION

SELECT the code AS a.code, a.name Name AS, COUNT (b.Ncode)

OD cdmaster a, nmmaster b

O a.code = b.code

And a.status = 1

And b.status = 1

And b.Ncode<> 'a10'

I TRUNC (last_update_date)> TRUNC (sysdate-13)

GROUP BY a.code, a.name;

Oracle UNION allows you to count according to a set of criteria.

TRUNC (last_update_date) <= TRUNC (sysdate-13)

He likes to count according to another set of criteria.

TRUNC (last_update_date)> TRUNC (sysdate-13)

The UNION ALL SQL statement is used to combine a result set of 2 or more SELECT comments. It does not delete duplicate rows between different SELECT accounts (all rows are returned).

Each SELECT entry in UNION ALL must have the same amount of fields in the feedback sets with the same data types.

What is the difference in amount in UNION and UNION ALL?

UNION deletes duplicate rows.

UNION ALL does not delete double lines.

The syntax

The syntax for UNION ALL in SQL is as follows:

SELECT expression1, expression2,expression_n

OF tables

[SO conditions]

UNION ALL

SELECT expression1, expression2,expression_n

OF tables

[WHERE conditions];

Parameters or arguments

expression1, expression2, expression_n

The columns or budgets that you want to resend.

Tables

Tables from which to extract records. There must be leastways for one table listed in the FROM clause.

Where are the conditions?

Optional. Conditions to be fulfilled for the selection of the recordings.

Note

There must be the same number of expressions in both SELECT expressions.

Matching expressions must have the same type of data in SELECT comments. For example, expression1 must be of the same data type in the first and second SELECT statements.

See also, the UNION operator.

Example: A field with the same name.

Let's see how to use the UNION ALL SQL operator to return a field. In this part, the field in both SELECT statements will have the same name and type of data.

For example:

SELECT provider_id

FROM the service provider

UNION ALL

SELECT provider_id

OF commands

ORDER BY Vendor_id;

This SQL UNION ALL example would return Supplier_id multiple times in the result set if the same value appeared in both the vendor table and the command table. The UNION ALL SQL statement does not remove duplicates. If you want to remove duplicates, try a UNION operator.

Now, let's explore this example in detail.

If you have filled the vendor table with the following records:

supplier_idsupplier_provider

1000 Microsoft

2000 Oracle

3000 apples

4000 Samsung

And the command table is populated with the following records:

order_idorder_datevendor_id

1 2015-08-01 2000

2 2015-08-01 6000

3 2015-08-02 7000

4 2015-08-03 8000

And he made the following statement from UNION

ALL:

SELECT provider_id

FROM the service provider

UNION ALL

SELECT provider_id

OF commands

ORDER BY Vendor_id;

You will get the following results:

Vendor identification

1000

2000

2000

3000

4000

6000

7000

8000

As you can see in this example, UNION ALL retrieved all value_id values from the vendor table and the order table and returned a combined result set. Duplicates have not been removed, as shown by the value of the 2000 vendor, which appeared twice in the result set.

Example: Different field names.

The corresponding columns of each SELECT command do not need to have the same name, but must have the same relevant data types.

When you do not have the same column names between SELECT statements, it becomes a little complicated, especially when you want to sort the results of a query using the ORDER BY clause.

Let's see how to use the UNION ALL operator with different column names and sort the results of the query.

For example:

SELECT provider_id, provider name

FROM the service provider

WHERE donor_id> 2000

UNION ALL

CHOOSE the name of the organisation, the name of the organisation.

OF companies

WHERE company_id> 1000

ORDER UP TO 1;

In this example, SQL UNION ALL operator because the column names are different between the two SELECT statements, it is better to call the columns in the ORDER BY command because of the position in the result set. In this example, we have sorted the results by vendor_id / company_id in ascending order, as shown in ORDER 1. The Supplier_id / company_id fields are in position 1 in the result set.

Explore this example with the data.

If you have filled the vendor table with the following records:

supplier_idsupplier_provider

1000 Microsoft

2000 Oracle

3000 apples

4000 Samsung

And a social table filled with the following documents:

Company Name

1000 Microsoft

3000 apples

Sony 7000

8000 IBM

And you made the following statement from UNION ALL:

SELECT vendor_id, vendor name

FROM THE SUPPLIER

WHERE vendor_id> 2000

UNION ALL

CHOOSE the name of the company, the name of the company.

Enterprises

WHERE company_id> 1000

ORDER UP TO 1;

You will get the following results:

supplier_idsupplier_provider

3000 apples

3000 apples

4000 Samsung

Sony 7000

8000 IBM

First, notice that a Supplier_id record of 3000 appears twice in the result set because the UNION ALL query returns all rows and does not remove duplicates.

Second, keep in mind that the column headers in the result set are called vendor_id and the provider name. This is because of the column names used in the first SELECT statement in UNION ALL.

If you wanted, you could have deleted the columns as follows:

SELECT provider_ID AS ID_Value, provider name AS Name_Value

FROM THE SUPPLIER

WHERE vendor_id> 2000

UNION ALL

SELECT Company_ID AS ID_Value, Company Name AS Name_Value

Enterprises

WHERE company_id> 1000

ORDER UP TO 1;

From now on, the column headings of the result will be alienated as ID_Value for the first column and Name_Value for the second column.

ID_VALUE NAME_VALUE

3000 apples

3000 apples

4000 Samsung

Sony 7000

8000 IBM

Combines the results of two queries into a result set. You control whether the result set includes double rows:

UNION ALL - Includes duplicates.

UNION - Excludes duplicates.

Operation UNION is different from UNION:

UNION links a set of results from two queries. But UNION does not create single rows from columns collected from two tables.

JOIN compares the columns of two tables in order to create rows of results composed of columns of two tables.

Here are the basic rules for combining a result set of two queries using UNION:

The number and order of columns must be the same in all queries.

Data types must be compatible.

The syntax

{<specification_query> | (<Consulta_expresión ')}

{UNION [ALL]

{<specification_query> | (<Consulta_expresión ')}

[... not]}

Arguments

<specification_query> | (<query_expression>), this is a query specification or query expression that returns data that will be combined with data from another query specification or query expression. Column definitions that are part of a UNION operation do not have to be identical, but must be supported by an implicit conversion. When the data types differ, the resulting data type is determined based on the priority of the data type. When the species are identical but differ in their precision, scale, or length, the result is based on the same combination of expression rules. See Precision, Scale, and Length (Transact-SQL) for more information.

The columns of the XML data type must be identical. All columns must be written in an XML schema or without writing. I wrote, and they must be written in the same collection of XML schemas.

UNION

Specifies that multiple result sets should be combined and returned as a result set.

ALL

Include all lines in the results, including duplicates. If not specified, the double lines are deleted.

Samples

Use simple UNION

In the following part, the result set includes the contents of the ProductModelID and Name columns in the ProductModel and Gloves tables.

SQL

- Use AdventureWorks

IF OBJECT_ID ('dbo.Gloves', 'U') IS NOT NULL

DROP STOL dbo.Guantes;

IR

- Make a glove table.

SELECT ProductModelID, Name

AND dbo.Guantes

DE Manufacturing.ProductModel

WHERE PRODUCTMODELID IN (3, 4);

IR

- Here is a simple union.

- Use AdventureWorks

SELECT ProductModelID, Name

DE Manufacturing.ProductModel

OR THE PRODUCT MODEL IS NOT IN (3, 4)

UNION

SELECT ProductModelID, Name

From dbo.Gloves

NAME ORDER;

IR

Using **SELECT INTO** with **UNION**

In the following example, the INTO sentence of the second SELECT statement specifies that a table named ProductResults contains a set of final merge results for the selected columns of the ProductModel and Gloves tables. The glove table was created in the first SELECT statement.

SQL

- Use AdventureWorks

IF OBJECT_ID ('dbo.ProductResults', 'U') IS NOT NULL

DROP TABLE dbo.ProductResults;

IR

IF OBJECT_ID ('dbo.Gloves', 'U') IS NOT NULL

DROP STOL dbo.Guantes;

IR

- Make a glove table.

SELECT ProductModelID, Name

AND dbo.Guantes

DE Manufacturing.ProductModel

WHERE PRODUCTMODELID IN (3, 4);

IR

- Use AdventureWorks

SELECT ProductModelID, Name

In dbo.ProductResults

DE Manufacturing.ProductModel

OR THE PRODUCT MODEL IS NOT IN (3, 4)

UNION

SELECT ProductModelID, Name

OD dbo.Gloves;

IR

SELECT ProductModelID, Name

OD dbo.ProductResults;

Using the union of two SELECT statements with ORDER BY

The order of the individual parameters used with the UNION clause is essential. The following example shows the correct and incorrect use of UNION in two SELECT statements in which the name of the column in the output is changed.

SQL

- Use AdventureWorks

IF OBJECT_ID ('dbo.Glovess', 'U') IS NOT NULL

PUT DOWN CHART dbo.Glaves;

To go

- Create a glove table.

SELECT ProductModelID, Name

EN dbo.Guantes

Production Product Model

OR BETWEEN THE PRODUCT (3, 4);

To go

/ * INCORRECT * /

- Use AdventureWorks

SELECT ProductModelID, Name

Production Product Model

WHERE THE PRODUCTODELID IS NOT IN (3, 4)

ORDER BY NAME

UNION

SELECT ProductModelID, Name

OD dbo.Gloves;

To go

/ * IT'S CORRECT * /

- Use AdventureWorks

SELECT ProductModelID, Name

Production Product Model

WHERE THE PRODUCTODELID IS NOT IN (3, 4)

UNION

SELECT ProductModelID, Name

OD dbo. Gloves

ORDER BY NAME

To go

Using the UNION of Three SELECT Statements to Show the Effects of ALL and Parentheses

The following examples use UNION to unite the results of three tables that contains the same five rows of data. The first example uses UNION ALL to display duplicate records and returns the 15 rows. In the second example, UNION without EVERYTHING is used to eliminate duplicate rows from the combined results of three SELECT statements and return five rows.

The third sample uses ALL with the first UNION, and the brackets place the second with UNION without using ALL. The second UNION is progress first because it is in parentheses and restores five lines because ALL options are not used, and duplicates are removed. These five lines are combined with the results of the first selection using the keywords UNION ALL. This example does not delete the copies between two sets of five lines. The final result has ten tracks.

SQL

- Use AdventureWorks

IF OBJECT_ID ('dbo.EposleeeOne', 'U') IS NOT NULL

DROP TABLE dbo.EEmployeeOne;

To go

IF OBJECT_ID ('dbo.EslueeeTwo', 'U') IS NOT NULL

DROPS TABLE dbo.EslueeeTwo;

To go

IF OBJECT_ID ('dbo.EEmployeeThree', 'U') IS NOT NULL

DROP TABLE dbo.EEmployeeThree;

To go

SELECTION pp.LastName, pp.FirstName, e.JobTitle

IN dbo.EEmployeeeOne

FROM PERS.Person AS pp JOIN HumanResources.E AS Employees and

ON e.BusinessEntityID = pp.BusinessEntityID

WHERE Name = 'Johnson';

To go

SELECTION pp.LastName, pp.FirstName, e.JobTitle

IN dbo.EEmployeeewo

FROM PERS.Person AS pp JOIN HumanResources.E AS Employees and

ON e.BusinessEntityID = pp.BusinessEntityID

WHERE Name = 'Johnson';

To go

SELECTION pp.LastName, pp.FirstName, e.JobTitle

IN dbo.EEmployeeThree

FROM PERS.Person AS pp JOIN HumanResources.E

AS Employees and

ON e.BusinessEntityID = pp.BusinessEntityID

WHERE Name = 'Johnson';

To go

- Union ALL

SELECTION Name, First Name, Position Title.

FROM dbo.EEmployeeeOne

UNION ALL

SELECTION Name, First Name, Position Title.

DE dbo.EEmployeeewo

UNION ALL

SELECTION Name, First Name, Position Title.

DE dbo.EEmployeeThree;

To go

SELECTION Name, First Name, Position Title.

FROM dbo.EEmployeeeOne

UNION

SELECTION Name, First Name, Position Title.

DE dbo.EEmployeeewo

UNION

SELECTION Name, First Name, Position Title.

DE dbo.EEmployeeThree;

To go

SELECTION Name, First Name, Position Title.

FROM dbo.EEmployeeeOne

UNION ALL

(

SELECTION Name, First Name, Position Title.

DE dbo.EEmployeeewo

UNION

SELECTION Name, First Name, Position Title.

DE dbo.Eee employees

)

To go

Samples: Azure Synapse Analytics (SQL DW) and Parallel Data Warehouse.

Using a simple union

In the following part, the result set includes the contents of the CustomerKey columns of the FactInternetSales and DimCustomer tables. As the ALL keyword is not used, duplicates are excluded from the result.

SQL

- Use AdventureWorks

SELECT customer key

Internet sales

UNION

SELECT customer key

From DimCustomer

CUSTOMER ORDER BY CLIENT;

Using two SELECT UNION statements with ORDER BY

When a SELECT report of a UNION statement contains an ORDER BY command, this clause must be placed after all SELECT comments. The following sample extensively shows the correct and incorrect use of UNION in two SELECT statements in which the column is sorted with ORDER BY.

SQL

- Use AdventureWorks

- NEED

SELECT customer key

Internet sales

CUSTOMER ORDER

UNION

SELECT customer key

From DimCustomer

CUSTOMER ORDER BY CLIENT;

- CORRECT

USE AdventureWorksPDW2012;

SELECT customer key

Internet sales

UNION

SELECT customer key

From DimCustomer

CUSTOMER ORDER BY CLIENT;

Using two SELECT UNION statements with WHERE and ORDER BY

The following sample shows the correct and incorrect use of UNION in two SELECT statements where WHERE and ORDER are required.

SQL

- Use AdventureWorks

- NEED

SELECT customer key

Internet sales

Where key key> = 11000

CUSTOMER ORDER

UNION

SELECT customer key

From DimCustomer

CUSTOMER ORDER BY CLIENT;

- CORRECT

USE AdventureWorksPDW2012;

SELECT customer key

Internet sales

Where key key> = 11000

UNION

SELECT customer key

From DimCustomer

CUSTOMER ORDER BY CLIENT;

Use the UNION of three SELECT statements to display the effects of ALL and parentheses

The following examples make use of UNION to combine the results from the same array in order to show the effects of ALL and brackets when using UNION.

The first example uses UNION ALL to display duplicate records and returns three rows in the original table three times. Another example uses UNION without ALL to remove duplicate rows from the combined results of three SELECT statements and returns only non-duplicate rows from the original table.

The third example uses ALL with the first UNION and parentheses covering the second UNION that ALL do not apply. The second UNION is treated first because it is in parentheses and it returns only row in the table that is not duplicated because the ALL option is not used, and duplicates are removed. These lines are combined with the results of the first CHOICE using the keywords UNION ALL. This example does not delete the copies between two games.

SQL

- Use AdventureWorks

SELECT CustomerKey, First Name, Last Name.

From DimCustomer

UNION ALL

SELECT CustomerKey, First Name, Last Name.

From DimCustomer

UNION ALL

SELECT CustomerKey, First Name, Last Name.

OD DimCustomer;

SELECT CustomerKey, First Name, Last Name.

From DimCustomer

UNION

SELECT CustomerKey, First Name, Last Name.

From DimCustomer

UNION

SELECT CustomerKey, First Name, Last Name.

OD DimCustomer;

SELECT CustomerKey, First Name, Last Name.

From DimCustomer

UNION ALL

(

SELECT CustomerKey, First Name, Last Name.

From DimCustomer

UNION

SELECT CustomerKey, First Name, Last Name.

From DimCustomer

)

SQL JOIN

First, it helps to understand how databases store data. They use tables with rows and columns. Each line is a single record containing the same types of data, each stored in a column. For example, a customer information table might provide columns with the name, last name, and customer ID (unique for each customer, for example, to separate two John Smith). In this table, when a new user is added to the database, the new row is combined with a unique ID, along with his first and last name in the corresponding column.

Then, it is useful to know that the data can be extracted from the database using a short and structured query language or a SQL structure (see-kwul). Different types of databases (Oracle, Teradata, SQL Server, etc.) have their SQL syntax, but are generally similar.

All forms of SQL allow you to easily retrieve data from one or more tables in a result set, and all will enable you to join multiple tables.

For example, in addition to the customer table mentioned above, there could be a customer address table. This table could include a column for the address, one for the city, one for the country, and one for the compression and identification of the address (a unique number for each class). And to maintain this simplicity, although you rarely design such a database, it would also include the ID of the client whose address is in this record.

In this way, you can write a query that selects the name and information of a client table and associates a client table with a client address table, using a syntax that is similar to the following:

Select * from the customer, customer address

wherecustomer.cust_id = customer_address.cust_id

(*) Then return all records. The records come from the customer table and the customer address table. Therefore, each returned row will have all the columns of the user table and the user address table:

Name, cust_id, address, city, country, zip code, address_id, cust_id

Note the "where" clause in the previous query. This specifies the ONLY record combination in the Customer_address table of the user table to which cust_ids corresponds. This is the right way to join.

Cartesian merge, also known as product association, results in all records in one table joining all files in another. In the previous example, we can create a Cartesian merge by eliminating the 'Where' clause.

Suppose that there are 200 records in the customer table and each customer has a career in the customer address table (hence, another 200 records in the customer address table). If the query uses the correct syntax to merge the two tables, the result set must have 200 rows, and one row per user also contains address information.

However, if we delete the where clause, SQL returns

EACH the client associated with the EACH address. Customers 1 will have a record for Class 1, Address two and Address 3, etc. To address 200. Also, customers 2, 3, etc. Up to 200 customers.

The result set should be 40,000 instead of 200. Each of the 200 customers would display 200 times and 200 * 200 = 40,000. That is why the Cartesian combination is also called product combination because it is a multiplication of records, not just a combination of files.

See the following statements:

- Internal connection to the USING clause.

SELECTION * IN TABLE 1 INTERNAL CONNECTION WITH SECOND TABLE b APPLICATION (column name).

- Internal union with ON clause.

CHOOSE * From the first to the inner JO, join the second b to a.somecolumn = b.anthercolumn

It counts

The general operation in SQL statements is the internal union. Identify and combine only rows in linked database tables when a match can be found in both tables. The condition is used to determine the association of the data stored in the addressed tables. The keywords ON or USING can be effectively used to determine the binding condition:

ON is used when the Relations column has a different name.

USING is used when the Relations column has the same name in both tables.

See the following examples:

- ON clause

SELECTION *

FROM TABLE A TO

INTERNAL UNIT table b

ON a.someColumn = b.otherColumn

- Use clause

SELECTION *

FROM TABLE TO

INTERNAL UNIT table b

APPLICATION (column name)

Internal Union, Interstate Union and Union

In MySQL, CROSS JOIN AND JOIN stands for INNER

JOIN. The ANSI SQL standard describes CROSS JOIN as an unconditional union. It is a Cartesian product of two tables and it is called a cross union. In MySQL, it's just an internal stateless union. The result set is a Cartesian product of these tables.

If you want MySQL to create a Carthusian product with two tables, use the CROSS JOIN keywords to indicate this intent. It allows you to read your statement and manage your transfer code between different relational database management systems (RDBMS), such as Oracle or Postgres.

More than one alliance

It is not uncommon to combine multiple tables with a single statement, and nothing special. Just add combinations and conditions (most likely):

- More than one

SELECTION *

FROM TABLE TO

INTERNAL UNIT table b

ON a.someColumn = b.otherColumn

INTERNAL UNIT table c

ON b.anotherColumn = c.nextColumn

MySQL creates a large set of results in the first two steps. The first step is to combine rows of tables and tables. In the second step, the rows of tables and tables are combined.

Unbalanced link conditions in database queries

Relational database management systems or RDBMS use queries to extract data from the database. Queries can be built into multiple tables using equi or non equi merge. Queries can also specify where the conditions are, where the data will be retrieved under certain conditions, such as Choose student's student name where place_of_residence = "Chennai." The binding terms are specified as follows: Select a.client_name, b.id of the client a, an order b where a.cid of the client = b.cid of the client.

In the previous case, the connection is established between two tables and the command. Before running the query, the SQL engine calculates the execution plan. The query execution plan is a series of steps that are applied to determine the query optimizer. These steps would result in a series of operations that would reduce the costs of running the query. In complex situations, when queries are built between multiple tables that specify many conditions, one or two lost union states may result in longer execution times if the database contains a large amount of data.

The junction of two tables without junction conditions is only a network product of the two groups. If Table A has 10,000 rows, and Table B has 5,000 rows, the cross product of both tables will generate 5.00 million records. While, if a link condition is entered, the result set will contain 10,000 rows or 5,000 rows in the search results. If a query includes, for example, ten tables and network products of two or three tables taken simultaneously, and the query expression contains 20 to 30 unions, then 3 or 4 links conditions may be lost due to negligence or error. This can happen in the case of SQL queries that run on a large production or production outputs that handle large amounts of data. The size of each table is enormous, as is the number of tables.

The designer can configure a query to record the update process in a production house where the actual sales data related to projections is loaded into the database. Because of the complexity of the database, a query can use 20 tables with an average of more than 100,000 records per table. The query can use many combinations, and if due to an accident, some link conditions are ignored, the query will search in the space of 10 power records instead of five power records. This would result in longer execution time of the query. Sometimes a program that contains an incorrect request may run for up to 20 hours without updating, but if lost queries can be identified and added to the query, such as table3.column3 = table4.column7 or table7.column2 = table1.column9, and so on, they can be executed within acceptable time frames.

CHAPTER NINE

Difference between function and stored procedure

What is a stored procedure (SP)?

A stored procedure is a set of queries/commands encapsulated in a function that is stored on a database server. The service can receive parameters that can then be used as request/command parameters.

Why is a stored procedure useful?

Because SP will tailor your queries/commands to parameterised data queries/data definitions/changes, you can standardise the exchange of data between the database server and its users. This will also reduce the debug time of application development because all business logic is stored in the database. The SP can help you maintain security by classifying authorised and forbidden users to call stored processes.

Why do we need a stored procedure?

Since we want to achieve the result mentioned in number 2, we can simply do this by replacing the stored procedure as a function library stored outside of the database server. But this will interfere heavily with the flexibility of the type of applications that makes use of the same business logic. For example, the current business application uses an Internet interface; if we want to create a smartphone/desktop-based client application, we will use more time to translate business logic into different programming languages/frameworks. We will have a terrible headache if we have to update the application, but not the business logic.

Why do not we need a stored procedure?

Because SP is less potent than the programming language used in a web application/business application/smart client, it is also possible that we are locked into a single RDBMS provider. As a result of which we are reducing flexibility in managing our IT budget.

When is the registered process appropriate for us?

When you are sure that the current RDBMS will be implemented in your organisation long enough for the time needed to develop the stored procedure, then extending the program to multiple platforms/programming language should be mentioned in your application development plan.

Stored procedure data

The use of stored procedures to consider has several advantages. This technology offers the power of a precompiled execution. The example shows the SQL server that compiles each method and then reuses the executed plan to improve performance when system calls are repeated dramatically. Also, the client or server traffic is reduced. If you give high priority to network bandwidth, you should be satisfied because you can minimise single-string SQL queries sent over a cable.

Also, another feature of stored procedures is the efficient reuse of programs and code abstraction. Multiple users or client programs can apply the technology used for stored procedures. If you use them in an organised plan, you will probably realise that the development cycle is faster. There are also enhanced security controls because you can grant permissions to users so that they can run the process themselves without any leaves from the table.

Stored procedures looks a bit like other types of programming language, such as user-defined functions. Also, SQL Server supports other temporary methods, such as temporary tables, in which they are automatically ignored when the connection is disconnected. These transient processes are in "tempdb" and maybe viable for earlier versions of SQL Server. They can be used with the application to create dynamic Transact-SQL statements.

Instead of asking Transact-SQL statements to recompile each interval, this stored procedure allows you to create a temporary built procedure on first performance before running the precompiled plan multiple times. However, continuous or tight clothing may eventually cause the system cards to be transferred to "tempdb". Also, the procedures provide native support for the OLE DB and ODBC model executed without using stored procedures.

Comparing Functions and Procedures Stored in SQL Server

1. Handling results of stored procedures and functions with table values.

To store the extracted data from a stored process in a table when we call it, you must first create a table and then insert the process data that is stored in the table.

Let's look at a sample. We will first create a stored procedure that returns the selected expression:

Create a sample of a process table

as

to choose

[AddressID]

[Address1,]

[AddressLine2]

1 C

of

[Nobody]. [Address]

This is a procedure called sample table, and returning the selection of information from the Person table to the address is included in the Adventureworks databases mentioned in the requirements.

After you create a stored procedure, you must create a table to store the data in:

CREATE A TABLE [Person]. [Address2] (

[Address ID] [int] NO NULL,

[AddressLine1] [nvarchar] (60) NO NULL,

[AddressLine2] [nvarchar] (60) NULL,

[City] [nvarchar] (30) NO NULL

CONSTRAINT [PK_Address_AddressID2] CLUSIFIED PRIMARY KEY

(

[AddressID] ASC

)

) ON [PRIMARY]

IR

Finally, you can insert in the table and call the stored procedure:

Insert into a person.Address2

An example of an executable table.

As you can see, the stored procedure can be called and extracted by inserting it.

If we try to insert from a stored procedure to automatically create a table, we get the following result:

An example of an executable table in

Address of the person3

When you try to insert the result of calling a stored procedure in a table, the following message is displayed:

Message 156, Level 15, State 1, Line 170

Incorrect syntax near the "en" keyword.

Let's create a function with table values and compare it to the stored procedure:

CREATE FUNCTION dbo.functiontable ()

RETURN TABLES

How? 'Or' What

Vraca

(

to choose

[AddressID]

[Address1,]

[AddressLine2]

1 C

of

[Nobody]. [Address]

)

This function called the function table, returns information about the person. Address table To call a function with table values, we can make a selection like this:

Select *

withdbo.functiontable ()

A function with table values can be used as a view. You can filter the columns that you want to see:

selectAddressID

withdbo.functiontable ()

You can also add filters:

selectAddressID in dbo.functiontable ()

whereaddressID = 502

If you want to store the outcome of a function, you do not need to create a table. You can use the select clause in the class to store the results in a new table:

Select *

at my table

withdbo.functiontable ()

2. Comparison of the performance of procedures and functions stored in the value of the table with the clause where

Some developers claim that stored processes are faster than table-based services. Is it true?

We will create a table of one million rows for this test:

With random values

as (

select 1 id, CAST (RAND (CHECKSUM (NEWID ())))) * 100 as integer) random number

union all

select id + 1, CAST (RAND (CHECKSUM (NEWID ())))) * 100 as integer) random number

random values

or

id<1000000

)

Select *

in my big

random values

OPTION (MAXRECURSION 0)

The code creates a table called my large table of millions of rows with values between 1 and 100.

We will create a function that returns values against a filter that is specified by a parameter:

CREATE FUNCTION dbo.functionlargetable (@rand int)

RETURN TABLES

AS

Return

(

select a random number

from my big office

where random number = @ rand

)

3. Are scalar functions bad?

Some say that scalar functions are an offshoot of the devil. We will check if this bad reputation is justified.

We will use a stored procedure with a computed column. The calculated column will convert US dollars to Mexican pesos. The formula will be:

Select a random number * 20.33 [Mexican pesos]

$ 1 will be 20.33 pesos.

The stored procedure will be as follows:

Create a grand table procedure

as select a random number * 20.33 [Mexican pesos]

from my big office.

We use the table that created my big table in section 2.

To test the results, we can refer to the following procedure:

Largetableproc executive.

The fast development of database applications.

A fast database application revolves around the concept of identifying and using fast and straightforward database applications. Here are some examples of such software that you can use, so keep reading.

There are many reasons why you need a fast connection to the database. For example, when you develop a custom database to manage your business data or need a quick update of the eCommerce site, it will help you to reduce downtime during updating of your website.

To produce the best application, you must specify the user interface design, the database design, the business strategy treatment design, the test plan, and the implementation process. You must also have a training plan and all the necessary material plans, i.e. implementation/acquisition plans, database standardisation, stored procedures and triggers.

Now, you must create a preliminary database design and use a modelling tool to test all database indexing structures. This will allow you to quickly develop database applications when you move to "mass production" or massive scale development.

When you want to get dirty at work, you can use the MSSQL, MySQL, Oracle, Alpha Five or Access databases. Some other newer development technologies include C #, ASP.NET, and VB.NET.

Samples of fast or fast database application development tools now include the Base One Foundation Component

Library (BFC), which you can use to build .NET applications using SQL databases. Server, Oracle, DB2, Sybase and MySQL. Others include Clarion, Developers and Construction, which is a tool and development environment for fast Windows and Web business applications for the .NET framework.

CHAPTER TEN

SQL Encrypting

Microsoft SQL Server users are asking us whether they should always use encrypted or transparent data encryption to use secured and confidential information. This is a relevant issue, especially given the concerns of the GDPR, and it is suitable for many other compliance and data requirements regulations. Let's dig into these technologies in more detail, and I think a response will be given.

Always Encrypted

Always Encrypted is a comparatively new client-side implementation of SQL Server encryption. That is to say that the data is encrypted on the source system before being inserted into the SQL Server database. Run as a Windows driver, Always Encrypted intercepts your SQL statement before exiting the client-side system (computer, web server, etc.), determines if there are fields in the SQL statement to be encrypted, establishes or retrieves an encrypted key, encrypts the domain and sends a modified SQL statement to SQL Server for processing.

An advantage of this approach is that the data is encrypted when moving in an internal or external network and stored in a database. Recovering encrypted data cancels this process by ensuring that information is protected in transit.

An essential limitation of Always Encrypted is that it can only be applied to a small subset of SQL operations. Many SQL operations are complex and cannot be processed as Always Encrypted.

Transparent encryption of data and encryption at the cellular level

SQL Server Transparent Data Encryption (TDE) and Station Level Encryption (CLE) are server-side objects that encrypt the entire SQL Server database on hold or the selected columns. The client-side application completely ignores the TDE or CLE implementation, and no software is installed on the client-side system. The SQL database itself performs all the encryption tasks. It is quite easy to implement and it works very well for most SQL Server users.

TDE and CLE are part of Microsoft's SQL Server key management strategy, which has been part of the SQL Server since it was launched in 2008. This technology is well developed, and many companies use TDE or CLE to protect their confidential data.

Manage encryption keys

Encryption policy is as valid as your encryption key management policy. Creating, protecting, and utilised encryption keys are a difficult part of encryption. For your overall security, the correct management of your keys are essential.

Transparent data encryption is a crucial well-defined management strategy through the Microsoft Extensible Key Management (EKM) provider interface. Critical management systems, such as our Alliance Key Manager for SQL Server, provides written software with the EKM interface specification, and SQL Server users can achieve complete management of the built-in encryption key through the interface of EKM supplier.

Always encryption does not provide a crucial formal management interface. Instead, external providers must always offer encrypted drivers that implement the interface in the key management system. This means that the key management system interface is proprietary. Also because the implementation is always a client-side encrypted implementation, each client-side application must have access to the key manager in order to protect and use the encryption keys properly. This can be a challenge for distributed network topologies.

In a nutshell: you can get critical management of any approach, but expect to find yourself more complex with Always Encrypted when distributing clients.

When to use always encrypted

Since the Always Encrypted functions modify the SQL operation before interacting with the SQL Server database, and many complex SQL operations will not work with Always Encrypted, I would still recommend using Encrypted only when the architecture of L application is simple. For example, you can use data that is always encrypted to send data from an internal SQL Server database to a database and SQL Server Web Hosting application. The data will be saved in transit and encrypted in the database. As long as your web application includes simple SQL queries in the database, this approach can work properly.

Transparent Data Encryption (TDE)

Transparent Data Encryption (TDE) encrypts data in physical database files, "inactive data." Without the original encryption certificate and the master key, the data cannot be read when accessing the device or stealing the physical media. The data contained in the unencrypted data files can be read by sending them to another server. TDE requires planning, but can be enforced without changing the database. Robert Sheldon explains how to apply the TDE.

With the release of SQL Server 2016, Microsoft extended the security features of the database engine by adding Transparent Data Encryption (TDE), which is a built-in feature for inactive data encryption. TDE protects physical media containing data associated with a user database, including data and log files, as well as backups or records. Inactive data encryption can prevent malicious people from reading them if they can access the files.

SQL Server TDE uses all or nothing against data protection. When enabled, TDE encrypts all information in the database, as well as many outside the database. You cannot select and choose how to proceed with the encryption at the column level. Nevertheless, it is relatively easy to activate TDE once you have successfully chosen the route to follow.

In this part, we will know how to implement TDE in a user database. The element is the second in a series on SQL Server encryption. The first (SQL Server Encryption: Using the Encryption Hierarchy to Protect Column Data) covers column-level encryption. If you know SQL Server encryption for the first time, you can first view the article.

TDE encryption hierarchy

When I introduced column-level encryption, I analysed the encryption hierarchy and how SQL Server uses several keys and certificates to protect column data. The approach used to implement the TDE is quite similar, but different enough to be strictly observed.

Similar to column-level encryption, the Windows Data Protection API (DPAPI) is at the top of the hierarchy. It is used to encrypt the Master Service Key (SMK), an asymmetric key located in the database. SQL Server creates SMK the first time an instance is commenced. Also, you can utilise the key to encrypt credentials, connected server passwords, and master database keys (DMKs) residing in different databases.

In the TDE encryption hierarchy, SMK is less than DPAPI and DMK less than SMK. The DMK is a symmetric key that is encrypted at the column level. However, using column-level encryption, you create a DMK in a user database in which the data in the column will be encrypted. Using TDE, you create a DMK in the master database even if it will encrypt the user database. SQL Server uses the user-supplied SMK words and password to encrypt the DMK with a 256-bit AES algorithm.

Before continuing with our description, take a close look at the following image that presents the entire TDE encryption hierarchy, starting with Windows DPAPI at the top and SQL Server data at the bottom. As you can see, the next level in our authority is the certificate, which is also created in the master database.

The DMK protects the certificate and the guarantee protects the database encryption key (DEK) in the user database. DEK is specific to TDE and is utilised to encrypt the data in the user database where the key is located.

You can ignore the DMK and the certificate as a whole, and use the Extensible Key Management Module (EKM) to protect the DEK key. SQL Server 2008 introduced the EKM framework as a way to store encrypted keys in hardware outside the database, essentially integrating hardware into encryption. However, this is an EKM problem that is beyond the scope of this part but would be addressed later in this series.

For the moment, we will direct you on the TDE encryption hierarchy as shown in the figure. We can conclude that the implementation of TDE in a database of users must be done and we must follow the following steps:

Create a DMK in the master database if it does not already exist.

Perform a check-in the central DEK insurance database.

Create a DEK key in a custom encryption database.

Enable TDE in the user database.

By actualising TDE, DBAs can meet the examiner's encryption necessities. To enable a database to utilise TDE, you can use the following step:

To do this, we will need to configure a test database similar to the one presented in the following T-SQL script:

USE the master;

To go

CREATE DATABASE EmpData2;

To go

USE EmpData2;

To go

CREATE EmpInfo TABLE (

PRIMARY KEY RECEIVED,

NatID NVARCHAR (15) IS NOT NULL,

LoginID NVARCHAR (256) NO NULL);

To go

PUT IN EmpInfo (EmpID, NatID, LoginID)

SELECTION BusinessEntityID, NationalIDNumber, LoginID

DE AdventureWorks2014.HumanResources.E Employee

O NationalIDNUM IS NOT NULL;

The database and table created here differ only slightly from those we created in the first part in this series. The database admit the EmpInfo table and uses the INSERT statement to retrieve data from the HumanResources.E Employee table in the AdventureWorks2014 database. However, I named the new EmpData2 database in case you want to keep the database of another article. (Note that I created all the samples in a local instance of SQL

Server 2016).

You do not need to use this database to test the examples in this article. If you want to use another one (and you can try it safely), rename the database name accordingly. However, you would want the database to remain small so that it won't be cluttered during the initial encryption process.

Make a DMK

To create a DMK file that supports a database that promotes TDE, follow the same steps as creating a DMK file to support one-column encryption, except for one crucial difference. You must make the key in the master database as present in the following T-SQL code:

USE the master;

To go

Create a master key

PASSWORD ENCRYPTION = 'pw1234!';

The CREATE MASTER KEY statement does not support optional arguments. We need to provide the password with the basic syntax. (Of course, we would like to use a stronger and more real password.)

To confirm that the DMK has been created, we can

request a revision of the sys.symmetric_keyscatalog:

SELECTION of KeyName,

symmetric_key_idKeyID,

Key_lengthKeyLength,

Algorithm_descAlgorithm key

OD sys.symmetric_keys;

_the keys;

The SELECT statement returns the results displayed in the following table.

Keyname

Key Identifier

Keyengeng

KeyAlgorithm

MS_DatabaseMasterKey

101

256

AES_256

MS_ServiceMasterKey

102

256

AES_256

Note that the results include both DMK and SMK. As noted above, SQL Server automatically creates SMK in the primary database. As you can see, both keys are based on the 256-bit AES encryption algorithm.

Create a certificate

The next step is to create a document in your initial database using the CREATE CERTIFICATE statement. In SQL Server, the license is a digitally signed database security that connects the public and private keys.

SQL Server encryption explained

Transparent Data Encryption in SQL Server protects inactive data by encrypting the database and log files on the disk. This works seamlessly for existing client applications, so they do not need to be changed when TDE is enabled. TDE utilise real-time encryption at the page level. Pages are encrypted earlier being written to disk without increasing the size of their data and log files, and pages are decrypted when read from memory. TDE is only available in the Enterprise section of SQL Server. This also works for Azure SQL Database, Azure SQL Data Warehouse, and Parallel Data Warehouse.

TDE encryption has a hierarchical structure with the Data Protection API (DPAPI) at the top of the hierarchy and it is used to encrypt the service key (SMK). You can use SMK to encrypt credentials, associated server passwords, and master database keys (DMKs) that reside in different databases. SQL DMK is a symmetric main that protects private certificate keys and asymmetric keys stored in databases.

SQL Server can yield self-signed certificates for use with TDE, or you can request a license from the CA (a most common approach). If you choose to enable TDE, you must save the document and the associated private key to the report. You must restore or attach the database to another SQL Server to obtain the desired result. If you enable TDE in another SQL Server database, the tempdb database is also encrypted. If you disable TDE, you must keep the certificate and private key because some parts of the transaction log may remain encrypted until you have a full stand-in.

TDE also demand a database encryption key (DEK), a key protected by an asymmetric certificate stored in a primary database, or an asymmetric key protected by a service that uses Extensible Key Management (EKM), such as Microsoft Azure Key Vault. The database backup files that TDE activates are encrypted with the DEK key. Therefore, a certificate protecting the DEK key must be available during restore operations.

Symmetric keys utilise the same password to encrypt and decrypt the data. Asymmetric keys use a password to encrypt the data (public key) and another password to decrypt the data (private key). You can use the CREATE CERTIFICATE command to create certificates, and the CREATE SYMMETRIC KEY and CREATE ASYMMETRIC KEY Transact-SQL commands to create database encryption keys.